PHILOSOPHERS AND FRIENDS

Also by Dorothy Emmet and published by Macmillan

Philosophers and Friends

Reminiscences of Seventy Years in Philosophy

Dorothy Emmet

Professor Emeritus in Philosophy
University of Manchester

Honorary Fellow of
Lady Margaret Hall, Oxford

Fellow Emeritus of
Lucy Cavendish College, Cambridge

Foreword by Bryan Magee

MACMILLAN

First published 1996 by
MACMILLAN PRESS LTD
Houndmills, Basingstoke, Hampshire RG21 6XS
and London
Companies and representatives
throughout the world

ISBN 0–333–67013–2 hardcover

A catalogue record for this book is available
from the British Library.

10   9   8   7   6   5   4   3   2   1
05   04   03   02   01   00   99   98   97   96

Printed in Great Britain by
The Ipswich Book Company Ltd

To my friends who are also philosophers

Niemals bin ich allein.
Viele, die vor mir lebten,
und fort von mir strebten,
webten,
webten,
an meinem Sein.

Rainer Maria Rilke.

I am never alone.
Many who lived before me
and many who strove away from me were
woven,
woven,
in my being.

Contents

List of Plates

1 Dorothy Emmet and Brian Magee in conversation at her 90th birthday party. Reproduced with the permission of D.H. Mellor.

2 A.D. Lindsay. Reproduced with the permission of Drusilla Scott.

3 A.N. Whitehead. Reproduced with the permission of the British Academy.

4 Samuel Alexander. Photograph by F.W. Schmidt. Reproduced with the permission of the University of Manchester.

Foreword

Many casual music lovers listen to music by none but the greatest composers. But serious music lovers are bound to find themselves exploring the work of lesser-known figures. Not infrequently some of this turns out to be better than its reputation, and may come to the fore afresh, and a reputation is then revised. The rest may continue to be seen, perhaps, as something less than great – but, even so, it is often full of talent, and capable of giving a great deal of pleasure, and will certainly add variety and interest to what would otherwise be a narrow diet. It provides us with a setting in which the greatest composers can be seen in better perspective. Without it the art of music would have nothing like the range and richness that it does.

I suppose something similar to this must be true in most important fields of human activity. Certainly it is in philosophy. The generally acknowledged 'greats' among philosophers, from Plato to Wittgenstein, are surprisingly few in number – I am talking of those of previous generations whose work one would unavoidably have to know if one were teaching philosophy at a university today. I doubt whether an honest reckoning could bring the number to more than about two dozen – and they (unlike the composers) would be spread over a period of nearly two and a half thousand years. Yet at every period there have been lesser figures, often many of them, whose work is of interest to the serious lover of philosophy, sometimes for a single insight, sometimes because it sparkles with many if smaller gems, or because it influenced one of the greater figures, or because it is well written – there can be any one of a number of sufficient reasons. Sometimes a new generation of readers will perceive that one of these has more to be said for him than has been realized, and his reputation will be re-evaluated – he may even be added to the company of the elect. And the rest will continue to deepen our appreciation of the past, and of the problem-situations out of which work of greater genius arose.

The supreme attraction of this book by Dorothy Emmet is that she brings alive, through the story of her personal connection with them, some of the most interesting philosophers of this kind who appeared in Britain during the half-century between the 1920s and the 1970s. She has good anecdotes to tell about some of them, and the stories often remind us how gifted they were – philosophers such as R.G. Collingwood, Samuel Alexander and Michael Polanyi. She also brings before us some of their most telling ideas with her usual clarity and penetration – she has a shrewd eye for what it is in the work of a past philosopher that is of interest to us now. For me a particular revelation is her account of the work of Samuel Alexander, of which I had been knowledgeless. And as is the case with every philosopher of whom she writes, she stimulates my interest not only in the philosophy but in the human being. Alexander, in addition to being a good philosopher, seems to have been a person of exceptional judgement. Not only did he see Frege as the greatest philosopher of his day, at a time when no one else seems to have done so, but it appears that when a foreign student in aeronautical engineering at Manchester, somebody called Wittgenstein, called to see him to talk over some problems about mathematics that were essentially philosophical, he advised the young man to go (and this meant travelling abroad) to visit Frege, thereby despatching him on a journey out of engineering and into philosophy that was to have epoch-making consequences. I find I want to know more about Alexander as a result of reading this book.

However, the member of Dorothy Emmet's cast of intriguing characters who seems to me the most promising candidate for a large-scale re-evaluation upwards is R.G. Collingwood (who, incidentally, described Alexander as 'a very rich, very wise and very profound thinker'). Collingwood had a low regard for the philosophy that was fashionable in his day, and never pretended otherwise. Since he got so little out of philosophical discussion with his colleagues he stopped engaging in it, and became the cat that walked by himself. This resulted in his being undervalued, and although he remains well known he remains also undervalued. In my opinion he is a better philosopher than all but a few of those who came after him, and the time has now come to reinstate him above those who mistakenly imagined they had superseded him.

Whitehead, who gets a chapter to himself, is another philosopher who, though unquestionably famous, is little known in the Britain of today as far as his actual work is concerned – especially that of the later period of his life, which is what Dorothy Emmet chiefly deals with. She has always been a leading exponent of this philosophy in Britain, and it is illuminating to read some of her second and third thoughts on the subject. Other equally large-scale figures make an appearance in what one might call cameo roles. Even on such a brief showing, though, they reveal their characters interestingly, and not always to the benefit of their reputations. We see yet again a Wittgenstein disregarding all considerations of relevance to focus the discussion on himself. We see a Popper who can be gentle and affectionate only after relieving himself of his own sting by releasing not one but two pent-up accumulations of acid.

No one who is seriously interested in twentieth-century British philosophers can fail to be interested in this book. In some cases the author is the only professional philosopher still alive who knew, personally, the people she is writing about: so she is our best link, and sometimes our only direct link, with that past. Her own career was unusual. When she became a student of philosophy at Oxford there were no tutors in the subject at any of the women's colleges, so she was taught at Balliol. As a professional philosopher she made a distinguished and distinctive contribution over a long period during which the profession contained very few women – my memory may be at fault here, but I can think of only one who became a Professor of Philosophy in Britain before her, and that was Susan Stebbing. In this book Dorothy Emmet is able to tell us from direct experience about a world very different from the one we are familiar with today. And the teller is as interesting as the tale.

Bryan Magee

Preface

This is not an autobiography nor an intellectual *apologia pro vita mea*. When I speak about events or about developments in my views, this will be incidental to describing how I have lived through a period of changes in philosophy. I shall not be giving anything like a history of philosophy during this period. If I were, the selection of philosophers would seem bizarre: why, for instance, discuss Prichard and Whitehead but not Moore and Russell, why include some who are not generally accounted philosophers? My principle of selection is to take those whom I knew and who made a personal impact on me. I shall bring in some – Popper and Wittgenstein for instance – with whom my contact was only occasional. But anecdotes from these occasions may be of interest in throwing light on some aspects of their complex personalities.

I have written whole chapters on three philosophers: Lindsay, Whitehead and Alexander. This may seem disproportionate but I have special reasons for recalling them and I would like to pass on something of what I got from knowing them. Lindsay was my philosophy tutor, and I find myself coming back to what I owe to him. Reading Whitehead's *Science and the Modern World* brought me seriously into philosophy; I have struggled intermittently over trying to understand him; people come and talk to me about him from time to time, and I thought I should give some estimate of how his philosophy looks to me now. I cannot claim any special knowledge or strong influence from Alexander, but he was the most beloved philosopher friend of the older generation, my predecessor but two in the Manchester chain, and it is a joy to remember him.

With one exception I have not written named sections on those now living, so my contemporaries have not needed to resort to attempts to steal the manuscript as P.G. Wodehouse in *Summer Lightning* tells us the Hon. Galahad's friends did when they found he was writing his memoirs. The exception in a named section is Alasdair MacIntyre. He was my one-time pupil; we collaborated on a book; and we have maintained intermittent but warm contacts over the years. I am glad to have a chance to discuss his recent views.

There are two to whom I want to give special thanks: Bryan Magee, who suggested that I should write this, and Derek Matravers who put my manuscript on his word processor and helped me with the copy-editing and proofreading. My qualification for writing is longevity. I have been in this game for over 70 years and seen changes in the ways in which it is played. And I am able to keep a toehold in some contemporary discussions.

Dorothy Emmet

1

Introduction

First, a few facts about my background. I was the eldest of three children of Cyril Emmet and Gertrude Weir. My father belonged to what is now probably an extinct species, the scholar country parson. We lived at West Hendred, a small village on the Berkshire Downs about 15 miles south of Oxford, in a vast vicarage, glorious in summer, bitterly cold in winter. It has now been renovated and sold as a gentleman's residence with central heating installed. As children we had to take our turn in sawing logs for open fires and pumping water for baths. So life was fairly austere physically, but this was more than offset by the joys of the garden, meadow, orchard and unspoilt countryside.

I did not go to school until I was nearly 14. We were taught by a not very intelligent governess, along with the children of other families in the neighbourhood. We were of different ages and stages, and the governess tried to keep us all going, sometimes by dictating from a row of books open in front of her, reading from them in turn, and you picked up from the one appropriate to you. But we were also taught by my father. He started me on Latin at the age of seven, and gave us Scripture lessons which partly consisted in showing us how the books of the Bible had emerged from a medley of different sources. So I never had to worry about discrepancies in the records; above all, he made us interested in discussing ideas – ideas about fundamental questions, or indeed about anything that came up. Also, he was fun. Religion was never something to be talked about in a special solemn tone of voice, separately from everything else. Moreover, the house was full of books; we read widely in English literature and talked about it. So my education was a matter of reading and talking rather than of formal instruction. There were big gaps, notably in science, which I have not succeeded in filling.

In 1918 my sister and I went to St Mary's Hall, Brighton. This was an endowed school for the daughters of clergy. It was said to have been a sister school of the one for clergy daughters behind that in

Charlotte Brontë's *Jane Eyre*. Life was fairly austere; again, there were gaps in our education, notably on the science side. On the arts' side the headmistress was a classical scholar with a keen sense for the meanings of words. When we wrote proses and did unseens, she insisted that English was as rich a language as Latin, indeed richer and we must not make do with one word where the other language had two. There must be the precisely right word in the right place. Not a bad background for philosophy, though I did not see it in that way at the time.

Rather endearingly, our headmistress combined a solemn demeanour with a gift for writing light verse and for constructing dramatic entertainments. For several years running we produced a variety performance showing episodes in the life of an imaginary village, Muddle-in-the-Marsh. One year it would be the School Outing, another the Choir Supper, and then the Village Concert. As clergy daughters, we knew plenty about these events, what happened in them and, more importantly, what could go wrong with them. It was not thought suitable that the vicar (MA Oxon et Cantab.) should appear, so he would have been summoned away, for instance to go to see the Archbishop of Canterbury. The Lady of the Manor, Lady Fitzpelham de Montague, was always present, in a large hat, with feather boa and lorgnette, the part being filled by our tall and stately headmistress. I was generally the village schoolmistress. We raised money by these performances to support a bursary for an adult student at the Working Women's College at Hillcroft – a very happy relationship.

So my schooldays, though patchy, were not unrewarding, and I went up to Lady Margaret Hall, Oxford, in 1923 to read Classical Honour Moderations and 'Greats' (*Literae Humaniores*); that is the honour school of philosophy and ancient history. We had then moved into Oxford from West Hendred, my father having been made Fellow and Dean of University College. He died just at the end of my last term at school. So I did not have the chance of talking to him about the philosophy I was doing in Greats. I think that this was when the religious interest with which I started, and which I have never quite lost, turned into an interest in trying to do philosophy. So this is where this story really begins.

2

Philosophy in Oxford in the 1920s: H.A. Prichard and R.G. Collingwood

Philosophy in the Oxford of the 1920s was in a very different world from that of philosophy in present-day Oxford, or indeed anywhere else. Wittgenstein's *Tractatus Logico-Philosophicus* was published in Ogden's translation in 1922, but no echo of it reached me. Nor did I hear of the Vienna circle. Cambridge philosophy, typified as that of Russell, was referred to as something to disagree with, except in the notable exception of the lectures of H.H. Price, who had worked as a post-graduate in Cambridge and brought back a strong influence from W.E. Johnson's *Logic*. I am glad to know that Price's papers are being republished with an Introduction by Martha Kneale. He has been underestimated.

There is a myth that the dominant philosophy in Oxford at that time was Absolute Idealism, but by the mid-1920s there were very few Absolute Idealists about. Bradley was still living until 1926, but he was a recluse in Merton; I never saw him and he certainly never lectured. H. Joachim lectured on Idealist Logic in beautiful prose, under the title of 'The Judgement'. He attacked the notion of truth as a property of propositions, each distinct from other propositions and from an external reality. No proposition could stand as true or false on its own; it had a background of presuppositions and implications. Judgement is a concrete piece of thinking made from within such a context which it seeks to probe. The goal would be to include all this context in a complete system which would surmount all oppositions, including that between mind and objects, and only this whole truth can be wholly true.[1]

I cannot say that I derived any very strong influence from Joachim. His book *The Nature of Truth* (Oxford, 1906) presents his views, probably the purest form of Idealism. His lectures on Logic, and

3

indeed the Logic paper in Greats, were in effect what would now be seen as epistemology, or even 'philosophy of mind' or what Ryle was to call 'informal logic'. Aristotelian syllogistic logic was represented by a paper in Mods., not, I think, often taken, and rather contemptuously called 'Mods. Logic'. Aristotelian Logic was indeed being developed in a sophisticated way by H.W.B. Joseph, but I did not put myself under his influence, to my loss as he might have helped me to acquire more badly needed precision. The Frege-Russell Logic never came our way.

On the whole the most distinctive type of philosophy in 1920s Oxford was a realist reaction to Idealism, mainly represented by the disciples of Cook Wilson. He was Professor of Logic in Oxford before the First World War and made a vigorous attack on the then dominant Idealism, somewhat in the manner of Moore but without Moore's rigour. He had something of an 'ordinary language' approach to problems, and indeed the term 'linguistic analysis' appears (for the first time?) in his *Statement and Inference* (Vol. II, p. 759).

H.A. PRICHARD

The realist philosopher with whom I had most contact was H.A. Prichard. Prichard combined a total dedication to getting things right with a narrowness of method which made it almost impossible for anything to pass muster as being right. Consequently he always seemed to be in a state of agonized worry. He lectured on 'the Object of Perception'; this ought to be something directly apprehensible as what it was. But what was it? Not a sense-datum, but a body in space, which must be indubitably there for us to apprehend. Prichard dismissed as pernicious nonsense the rising theories of quantum mechanics, where this cannot be said. Yet he always seemed to be unhappy about the object of perception. So was I.

But Prichard's influence came more in moral philosophy than in epistemology. In 1912 he wrote a paper in *Mind* which was to become something of a classic: 'Does Moral Philosophy rest on a mistake?' The mistake, from Plato to T.H. Green inclusive, was to centre on the concept of 'good' and to look at right actions as right in a context in which they were conducive to or expressive of what was good. Rather, we were much more sure that we had obligations to do acts of certain kinds than we could be sure of what could be meant by some elusive concept of good. So morality had nothing to do with teleological considerations and everything to do with the conscientious performance of intuitively evident obligations. These obligations were generalised in rules – for example keeping promises, telling the truth, assisting our aged parents if they need assisting. If people said that these obligations were not self-evident to them, this was a sign that they had not looked at them clearly, or perhaps that they had not been properly brought up.

Whatever the case about our upbringing, most of us, I think, found it hard to see morality built up piecemeal from evident obligations. If this was so in the 1920s, it is still less plausible in our contemporary moral complexities – over embryo research, abortion on demand, nuclear disarmament, to name no more. Prichard saw morality as applying a rule to do an action of a certain sort in situations of certain sorts. But a situation is constituted by the facts of the situation. Objectively one's duty would be to do what was right in the actual situation, and we can be mistaken about the facts of the situation; do we therefore have a subjective duty to do what we would see to be right in the situation as we believe it to be? ('Subjective' here referred to our possibly mistaken beliefs about the facts of situations. It did not entail any relativistic view as to the objectivity of what was really right.) The discrepancy between actual objective and possible subjective duty was a major source of worry for Prichard, a crack in the edifice of self-evident obligations. He agonized over it in his British Academy Lecture of 1932, 'Duty and Ignorance of Fact' and with relentless honesty came reluctantly to the conclusion that our obligation is to do what we subjectively believe would be right in the facts of a situation as we believe them to be. There was, I think, a further refinement: putative duty, which was to do what would have been objectively right had the situation been what we mistakenly thought it was. But this further refinement did not appear in 'Duty and Ignorance of Fact' which was concerned with the discrepancy between objective and subjective duty. This was sufficient worry for the British Academy Lecture. But in another sense, no worry was ever sufficient for Prichard. He would go on struggling to get something right. I was told however that there was one occasion on which he had to give up. He was viva-ing a large American in Greats, and he said 'Now, Mr So-and-so, you and I are shipwrecked on a raft and there is one small piece of bacon. How much would it be right for you to have, and how much would it be right for me to have?' The American replied 'I guess I would just wolf it all down and you too.' (Prichard was a very small man.) A shout of joy went up from the other examiners. But I do not want to mock Prichard. He was totally dedicated as well as painstaking. I sometimes hear him saying over my shoulder 'Don't hedge' when I am tempted to do so.

For Prichard, motives were morally indifferent, insofar as they involved desires, since desires were morally indifferent; what mattered was doing one's duty. This alone, unlike the conjuring up or cultivating of motives, was within one's power. I am told that a student in one of his classes said 'My old nurse used to say to me "Master Richard, you ought to try to be good".' Prichard rejoined 'She was confused.' One ought to do one's duty, this was not cultivating good motives; nor did he think that to do this was within one's power. What was strictly within one's power was not even to do an action of a certain kind. One might be paralysed while raising one's arm. All that is undoubtedly within one's power is to 'set oneself' to do a certain action, pressing the Kantian statement that 'ought implies can' to its limit.

Prichard may well have been right that this is all we can be certain of being able to do. But I think that where, for instance, a stroke prevents an action from being carried through, this would be more likely to be given as an excuse for a distressing failure to do one's duty than as a reason for saying that we had done it after all.

Another Oxford moralist of the time was W.D. Ross. He was more aware than Prichard of complexity in moral philosophy. Morality was less than it was for Prichard a matter of applying rules. Rules indeed were a generalization from judgements of what would be right in particular sorts of situation, and formulated through a kind of intuitive induction from these judgements. Such judgements were not infallible, but suggested *prima facie* duties. Ought one, for instance, to keep a promise or to betray a confidence? Hence there was a problem, not only over ignorance of fact, but over conflicting *prima facie* duties. In such cases which was the more stringent could not be deduced from general principles. It was incumbent on one to study the situation until one could form a considered opinion that in the circumstances one of these *prima facie* duties was the more pressing. This was itself an intuitive judgement and a fallible one. Ross, like Prichard, therefore thought that what one ought to do was what one subjectively but perhaps mistakenly judged to be right. This did not detract from the fact that what was really right was an objective matter.

If an action was right, this was because of some feature in virtue of which it was right. This could stem from something in the past – one had made a promise, for instance. Or it could be right as promoting some good. Ross was anti-Utilitarian in insisting that what was right was not an action done simply to promote one object as good such as happiness or interests. Several things were intrinsically good in virtue of certain attributes, and it was right to promote them. Those listed by Ross were virtue, knowledge, and within strict limits, pleasure. Moral goodness was a matter of motivation, of an agent doing something because he believed it to be right. There could also be goodness of character, of having a virtuous disposition to do what is right. Ross held, characteristically, that there was a duty to promote one's own moral improvement. He would have agreed with the nurse of Prichard's pupil. Goodness could therefore be an attribute of certain kinds of character or ways of feeling; this was the goodness of the agent, but emphatically not what made actions right.

Ross's views were given in his influential book *The Right and the Good* (1930) and more fully in the *Foundations of Ethics* (1939). (He had two daughters whom we called 'The Right' and 'The Good'.) Much of what he said abstractly about ethics, especially about *prima facie* duties, seemed sense. But his manner of lecturing was dry (he repeated each sentence at dictation speed), and his examples seemed far from what we might feel were pressing moral dilemmas. One of his problems, often quoted, was whether if you returned a borrowed book by post and it got lost, you had done your duty. Most of us would probably say you should send another copy and not argue about it.

Prichard's examples also seemed to show poverty in imagination of life. One which often recurs in the British Academy Lecture was whether if you came across an unconscious man by the roadside you should shout since you might think that if he had fainted shouting might revive him. There was the problem of ignorance of fact, as to whether he had indeed fainted, and also as to whether shouting would revive him. An elementary knowledge of first aid would surely have suggested that it would not. But I found Prichard's agonizing over his problems more appealing than the impression of secure rectitude which Ross made on me.

Both Ross and Prichard seemed to live in a very different world from that of moral problems as they actually impinged on us. A maverick philosopher who did seem to be living in our world was

John Macmurray. Since there appears to be a revival of interest in Macmurray, I shall write about him at some length, but in a later context since his main thinking about ethics came out in the 1930s rather than in the time when I knew him in Oxford in the 1920s.

R.G. COLLINGWOOD

Another maverick philosopher was R.G. Collingwood. He went his own way and in his *Autobiography* (Oxford, 1939) he pours scorn on the Oxford realist philosophers. His book *Speculum Mentis* came out in 1924, and I read it avidly, perhaps the more so for knowing how much it was disapproved of by our pastors and masters. Art, religion, science and history were distinct forms of thought going on under their own abstractions, while philosophy was the inclusive thought which overcame abstractions. I never quite believed this then, and I certainly do not do so now. Philosophy is not a sur-mounting of abstractions. It can indeed be a critical discussion of the abstractions used in any form of thinking, including its own. Any actual piece of philosophical thinking will have its own abstractions, even though using them critically. Any philosophy will still be a partial view. Collingwood himself put *Speculum Mentis* behind him and in 1933 he published *An Essay on Philosophical Method*. Here the pursuit of philosophy is integrally related to the history of philosophy. Philosophical thinking does not proceed deductively from clearly defined propositions. Its concepts are developed in their use at each stage by clarification and criticism of their former use, and this in its turn will be further clarified at a later stage. So an adequate definition of a philosophical concept, unlike one in math-ematics and, Collingwood thought, in science, would be given not at the beginning but at the end of an enquiry, if indeed there was an end. This book fell outside my Oxford period. I am calling attention to it because it contains a wealth of observation on what can be learnt philosophically from reading the history of philosophy, and that not only as history of ideas. This can well be lost in a time when the history of philosophy is often neglected, or pushed no further back than, say, to Moore and Russell. The view of philosophical method is also relevant to Rorty's contention that philosophy has been 'foun-dational', claiming to proceed from fixed starting points whether as propositions or sense data. For Collingwood what may be put forward as a starting point at any stage is open to re-assessment and re-definition in the light of what comes after. Collingwood sees the history of philosophy in these terms. I think there is a survival here of the Idealism which he claimed to have repudiated. It presents the history of thought as a continuous development carried out by thinking from inside the process where each stage overcomes limitations in the former stage. I question whether the history of thought can be as unified as this over time. I suspect that it is always likely to be carried on from different points of view with their differing assumptions.

Collingwood's next contribution to his view of how thought develops was given in *An Essay on Metaphysics* (1940). Here he described thinking as proceeding by giving answers to questions, where the answers are propositions. In all thinking there are certain background presuppositions and the most general of these he calls 'absolute presuppositions'. Metaphysics is the attempt to diagnose what these are in any period of thought. It is not a critique since what can be criticized are propositions which are answers to questions. Presuppositions are not propositions; they are not answers to questions, but assumptions that enable questions to be asked. But they can be abandoned, especially as science and history progress. Thus causation was an absolute presupposition in Newtonian Physics but abandoned in Relativity Physics. I am not sure whether presuppositions can be thus insulated from criticism. We find philosophers go on criticizing, dismissing, reinstating, reformulating the notion of causation. Again, Collingwood's views of the development of thought seems to make it appear more of a unity than it actually is.

I return to Collingwood's impact on me as an undergraduate. As a lecturer he was a spell-binder. I attended his course on the Philosophy of History, and the finished polish of what he was saying was such that I tried to scribble it down verbatim for consideration at a later time. I found my notes represented a preliminary version of what appeared in his book *The Idea of History*. Collingwood was indeed to produce a remarkable series of books (all published by Clarendon Press, Oxford), *The Principles of Art* (1945), *The Idea of History* (1946), *The Idea of Nature* (1945), interpreting Art, History and Science as forms of intellectual expression with a character peculiar to each. In the case of history, the aim is not to record facts; it is to re-enact the questions being asked by the actors in their situations, and to look for the answers in what they did. So all history becomes intellectual history, and so-called scientific history, for instance as studied through economic analysis, statistics, psycho-analysis, is pseudo-history. At best these studies can be subordinate ancillaries to the real history of how its participants saw questions and tried to answer them.

Collingwood himself, besides being a philosopher, was a historian of Roman Britain, and it is possible that this is a kind of history amenable to this method. The sources, at any rate at that time, were not very extensive, and were largely archeological – broken shards, sites of former buildings, encampments – and it would be plausible to interpret them by asking what kind of purpose they were for. This way of interpretation may be less plausible where the sources are more numerous and kinds of possible causation more diverse. For all its brilliance, Collingwood's view of history is over-intellectual, one could say over-rationalised. What about the factor of sheer contingency in courses of events, of happenings which cause the best designs of mice and men to go constantly agley?

Nevertheless, Collingwood was certainly one of the outstanding influences in philosophy between the wars, and it is good to hear that there is some revival of interest in him. There was an admirable lecture (unpublished) given by Simon Blackburn to mark the centenary of his birth. (Simon Blackburn held the Fellowship in Philosophy at Pembroke College, Oxford, which had been held by Collingwood in his day.) The lecture was called 'Wittgensteinian themes in Collingwood'; Blackburn shows how, like the later Wittgenstein, Collingwood rejected a view of atomic propositions, concatenated in theories, in favour of a view of propositions as having meaning through use in a context. Whereas for Wittgenstein the context is a form of life, for Collingwood it is given through question and answer within a particular situation. So a proposition is not abstracted from its history, and in the case of a philosophical proposition, this will be the history of philosophy within which it occurs as an answer to a question within that context. For Collingwood, to study history of philosophy, indeed any history, is to attempt to re-enact the thoughts and deliberations of the past. Wittgenstein does not set philosophy in its history – indeed, as is well known, he sat loose to the history of philosophy. His context is a form of life, in which people carry out practices according to rules. This context is less highly explicit than Collingwood's context in which they deliberate in a historical setting. But both were seeing thinking as a process in which people were participating, either with others in the present or as thinkers seeking to re-enact the deliberations of past participants.

I have put this in my own way: I hope it is fair to Blackburn's longer, and more subtle, presentation. What he has done in this lecture is to show that certain themes, which are nowadays sometimes spoken of as though they originated in the later Wittgenstein, can be found in Collingwood, though in a different form where attention is on the historical character of 'forms of life'. For Collingwood, history had now taken over from philosophy as the ultimate kind of thinking. However, for this to be acceptable 'history' must have a very wide meaning, so as to cover the sort of examples Wittgenstein gives of interpersonal engagement in practices.

Collingwood and Wittgenstein were both concerned with informal logic in practices and in historical thinking. Other models of more formalized kinds of thought, such as a mathematical theory connected hypothetico-deductively with propositions to be tested against facts, may come closer to scientific understanding and may not, as Collingwood claimed, be dependent on history. Or if it is said that the theory is an evolutionary one, that all nature is evolutionary, and evolution is a form of history, then it will be a kind of history very different from the human history in which people deliberate about their actions, where the Collingwoodian historian seeks to re-enact their deliberations in his own thinking.

In writing even briefly about Collingwood, I am aware of how he dismissed people who wanted to discuss his work: 'If there are any who think my work good, let them show their approval of it by attention to their own.'[2] Broadly, I agree that this is what one should do. But here I am taking the privilege of age to pay my respects to philosophers who have mattered to me, and Collingwood was one of these.

When I was at Oxford philosophy was part of two honour schools: one being *Literae Humaniores* ('Greats'), which combined philosophy and ancient history, the other being Philosophy, Politics and Economics ('Modern Greats'). Very few women took either, and there were no philosophy tutors in the women's colleges. I was tutored at Balliol, first by Charles Morris, then, as he was away in America for a year, by the Master, A.D. Lindsay. They had a very different style. Charles threw us about dialectically, putting views forward to see what we would say, and it was very difficult to discover what his own views were. Sandie Lindsay was concerned that we should be given the truth. This means that I missed something in critical precision and was not given the rigorous training I might have got in Cambridge or from some of the other Oxford philosophers such as Joseph. I have had since to try to remedy this. But I thought, still think, that the kind of views Lindsay gave us generally were the truth. His philosophy was not just, as is sometimes thought, a form of uplift, but a view which was full of good sense, and one which was not an ingrowing way of thinking, but which one could take into other concerns. Since his work is little known now, and since he is probably little read, I shall write about his views at some length.

Mrs Lindsay was also a person in my life. She was a poetess with a fine mind, high principles, and no time for small talk. On one occasion she invited my partner in tutorials, Sylvia Brown, and me to dinner 'to help us entertain the Eight' (the crew of the boat). It was the end of Eight's Week (the summer boat races) and the Balliol boat had done well. After dinner she collected us all together and read aloud from Doughty's *Arabia Deserta*. I don't know what the Eight made of it; perhaps like me they discovered Doughty.

3

A.D. Lindsay: Philosophy and Moral Democracy

Lindsay is mainly known as a political philosopher, and indeed *The Modern Democratic State* is likely to be his most enduring book. But he also had a strong interest in the theory of knowledge; here what he had to say, though it was never fully worked out, was not just an interest additional to his moral and political philosophy, but informed it. He had a way of looking at knowledge which drew first and foremost on Kant, but also very considerably on Bergson; on the more Socratic side of Plato, and on an interpretation of the Christian ideal of perfection. This suggests an eclectic collection of 'influences'; rather, reflection on these (as well as on his wide interests in literature) helped him to form a central set of convictions about thinking and action, which had its bearing on practical activities. Some, therefore, of the host of these which he undertook might be looked on as field work. Some, but not all; and they took so much out of him, especially in later life, that he never succeeded in producing a full and coherent statement of his own philosophical position. He may not have really wanted to do so; at any rate, what he left in writing was a number of variations on certain themes.

In his theory of knowledge: he stressed the importance of starting one's thinking from the possibility of error rather than from anything which is unquestionably true. He recalled how Socrates challenged sceptics by referring to the experience of craftsmen; there is a right and wrong way of building a ship or treating a patient. Similarly, in trying to judge what is true, we can be right or wrong; and in trying to do what we ought, we can be right or wrong. This is not a matter of 'mere appearance'; there is a real possibility of making mistakes. Mistakes are something we *make*, and making them is a form of action. Lindsay's theory of knowledge tried to take account both of our being active and indeed 'making something' in seeking to know, and also the independence of the realities we seek to know. So the

13

question asked in the title of his Presidential Address to the Aristotelian Society in 1924 was 'What does the mind construct?'. But long before that he was working on the principle that knowing starts from *action*, and not from 'apprehending' or contemplating indubitable starting points, whether sense data, or clear and distinct ideas, or axioms. He did not, as far as I know, ever look seriously at how what he believed about knowledge might be compared with Professor Ryle's views in *The Concept of Mind* (London, Hutchinson, 1949). I suspect that he would have approved of the emphasis laid on 'knowing how', or doing things intelligently, as a way of knowing. He would not have been happy about the minor role given to imagery; but he would surely have subscribed wholeheartedly to Ryle's remarks (op. cit., p. 238) that 'Ascertaining is not a process which bases upon a fund of certainties a superstructure of guesses; it is a process of making sure. Certainties are what we succeed in ascertaining, not things we pick up by accident or benefaction. They are the wages of work, not the gifts of revelation. When the sabbatical notion of "the Given" has given place to the week-day notion of "the ascertained", we shall have bade farewell to both Phenomenalism and the Sense Datum Theory.'

Whatever may happen in 'those endless Sabbaths the blessed ones see', week-day work is done in the body; and the starting point of knowledge for Lindsay is our power of initiating changes in the spatio-temporal world around us through our own bodies. Here he drew heavily on Bergson; his book *The Philosophy of Bergson* (London, Dent, 1911) already shows the main convictions which come out in his later work. Someone has said that the book on Bergson is in effect a good book on Kant. This might be countered by saying that Lindsay's 1934 book on Kant is in effect a good book on Bergson. Not that Bergson directly appears much in the latter book, though a remark of his that we need a Critique of non-Newtonian natural science is quoted with approval. Rather, what Lindsay seems to have done was to rub Kant and Bergson together in his mind, and approach them both through a view of knowledge which starts from thinking of ourselves as exploring a largely unknown world by acting on it through our bodies, noticing changes which we have initiated and comparing them with changes which we have not. This means that in interpreting Kant, Lindsay pushes him in the direction of empirical realism and away from phenomenalism (that is the view that knowledge can only be a connection of appearances). He claims support for the realist interpretation from the later revisions of the

Critique of Pure Reason, where the separation between 'inner sense', as experience of the empirical self in time, and 'outer sense', as experience of objects in space, is broken down, and each is shown to require the other. A case can be made that Kant was dissatisfied with the distinction of inner and outer sense; but Lindsay is bound to admit that Kant cannot be made to subscribe to the view that just as *freedom*, as the power to obey the categorical imperative, is necessary for morality, so freedom, as the power to initiate changes in the external world, is necessary for knowledge. This is the king-pin of Lindsay's own view; here he drew on Bergson rather than on Kant.

The main source is Bergson's *Matter and Memory*, and a good deal of Lindsay's book on Bergson is devoted to exposition of this. He was particularly impressed with the early part, where Bergson talks about the twofold role of the body. On the one hand our bodies are parts of a system of nature, changing and being changed through reciprocal interactions, like any other part of nature, according to the laws of a common external world. On the other hand, through our nervous system and sense organs, we are in a special relation to some selected parts of the external world, and they appear to alter according to changes and movements in our body. If we concentrate only on the body in its former role, consciousness becomes epiphenomenal and perception a mystery. If we concentrate only on the latter role, predictable outcomes of action in a common world become inexplicable and science a mystery. We need to start from our conscious experience of initiating action in a common external world. This might be said to be mere common sense; but it did not fit the prevalent contemporary forms of either Idealism or Realism; of Idealism because this was monistic and subjectivist; of Realism because this was based on what were held to be indubitable and incorrigible certainties, such as axioms in mathematics, obligations in morals, and coloured patches in perception.

Lindsay also appreciated Bergson's view of freedom, not only as something belonging to a moral self, but as a matter of degree, beginning in low form in the functional adaptiveness of living things. He wanted to see a Critique of the sciences of life, and thought that Bergson had begun to produce one. He also wanted to see a Critique of the historical sciences, and thought that Dilthey had begun to produce one. But though he called the attention of various people – notably H.A. Hodges – to Dilthey, it is doubtful whether he himself read further than the *Einleitung in die Geisteswissenschaften*.

Dilthey's notion of *Erlebnis*, experience as lived from within, has affinities with Bergson's Intuition, but is more systematically worked out and presented less romantically. Lindsay certainly believed in the importance of this kind of knowledge, but though he gives a sympathetic account of Bergson's notion of Intuition, he probably thought it was too far removed from criticism. At any rate he thought Bergson's separation of a self-sufficient inner experience, as an experience of time without space, produced the same sort of troubles as Kant's view of inner sense. Rather, he looked for an interplay between intuitive thinking and experimental action in a spatial-temporal world.

Lindsay was interested in the psychological side of Bergson's work. He says (*The Philosophy of Bergson*, p. 84 *n.*), 'It is somewhat startling to find Bergson describing facts as "images" but as his argument is not affected by any implications which might seem to be involved in talking about being in the presence of "images", I have omitted the word in my account.' Nevertheless, the word remains a difficulty; and this, or rather the problem of the status of 'images', comes up in Lindsay's one independent (that is non-commentary) paper on the nature of knowledge; the 1924 Aristotelian Society Address 'What does the mind construct?'

I have already said that, whatever Lindsay thought the mind constructed, it was not the object finally to be known. Yet he believed that something must be constructed – knowing is not simply a matter of being aware of something presented to us.

> Time and again philosophers impressed with the fact that in knowing we are faced with a reality which we not only do not make, but which our knowing does not alter, have tried to describe knowing as a process in which the mind is passive while things are active, or in which the mind's activity is at most one of pure contemplation or awareness, creating or effecting nothing except changes in itself, and time and again this attempt has broken down. For it has been impossible to ignore the fact that at least in error we are confronted with something which we have ourselves brought into being. (*Proceedings of the Aristotelian Society* 1924–5, p. 1)

This, of course, brought him into opposition to the forms of direct Realism which were strong in Oxford in the 1920s.

So we come to what is constructed, and this, Lindsay holds, is not something 'mental', but something in the physical world – as much in the physical world as other external realities. It may be a map; it may be a set of sounds in the air or marks on paper; it may be a chart showing the batting and bowling analysis of a game of cricket. It is something we make in a perfectly ordinary sense through bodily actions. It is symbolic, which means that it is something we use to help us understand something else. From his examples Lindsay would no doubt have been sympathetic to C.S. Peirce's view of 'iconic' signs, where there is some structural similarity between the symbolism and what is symbolized; but this similarity is not necessary. All that is necessary is that we should be able to distinguish the properties of the symbolism we have put in by our conventions, and the features in it which we vary according to how we observe the objects to which it is applied. The simplified construction is something we can grasp and manipulate in a way in which we generally cannot grasp and manipulate the complex things we are trying to understand.

So 'what the mind constructs' are *entia rationis* only in the sense that they are things made to serve the purposes of knowing; they are artefacts in the physical world which we make through our embodied actions. This seems straightforward so long as what is constructed is an honest-to-goodness artefact, such as a map. It is more difficult when Lindsay claims that he is also giving a generalized view of the place of 'images' in knowing, suggested by Plato in the *Sophist*, and that the making of 'mental images' is in principle the same as the making of maps, diagrams, or other aids to knowledge. One can perhaps see what he means when he says 'the construction by means of our psycho-physical organism of images we can be aware of and contemplate is not for logical purposes different from the construction of what Plato would have called images in the external world, maps, models, arrangements of symbols on paper or in succession of sounds' (op. cit., p. 18). But the stress here is on '*for logical purposes*' – an image is a *tertium quid* used to help us to think about something else. In using the term 'images' he distinguished those we construct through using our imagination, and which we can then contemplate, and those which are due to actions on our bodies by things in the external world. The latter are not something we deliberately construct and we are not always aware that we are using them as images (Lindsay also uses the term 'sensa'). However, we can tell they are partly conditioned by the state of our bodies because we can alter them by initiating changes in these, for instance by poking an eyeball. I think that nevertheless there is a certain ambiguity in his use of the term 'images' in these two ways.[1] In either case he is saying that to ask whether images are mental or physical is to make a false distinction. They occur in an organism which is part of the physical world, and we can use them for cognitive purposes or for aesthetic enjoyment. All this is sketched rather than worked out in anything Lindsay wrote. But the 'dualism' which he explicitly maintains is not a dualism of mind and matter but a distinction between changes in the world which we produce through our own bodily acts, and those which are either forced upon us or which we can see happening independently of the changes we initiate.

So actions and changes deliberately initiated in the external world, not separate data of which we are immediately and indubitably aware, are our starting point in considering how we come to know.

Here Lindsay's theory of knowledge, with the primacy it gives to action, owes as much to Bergson as it does to Kant. Yet he saw himself as nothing if not a Kantian. He wrote two books on Kant; a little one in Nelson's 'People's Books' series in 1919, and in 1934 a larger one, *Kant*, in Benn's 'Leaders of Philosophy' series. The former is a little masterpiece in popular exposition of a difficult philosophy. The latter was to have been Lindsay's definitive book on Kant. It contains some very good expositions, particularly in the historical account of Kant's background in philosophy and of his influence on various kinds of philosophy which came after him. It has not, however, really made a mark in Kantian literature. Lindsay is not the kind of commentator who puts the most literal interpretation on what Kant said, and then shows that it won't do; he interprets in the manner of someone who believes that what Kant was trying to say was broadly right, and that it can be sympathetically presented so as to appear sensible. This is an attitude to be applauded. But in the end the interpretation is considerably coloured by Lindsay's own experimental theory of knowledge as depending on action, and he surely underestimates Kant's phenomenalism and the extent to which the Kantian 'synthesis' is a mental process of ordering sensations, rather than creative activity in a common external world. His interpretation, however, comes most fully into its own when he applies it to the Reflective Judgement in the *Critique of Judgement*. In discussing the aesthetic and teleological judgement in the third Critique,

Kant now sees that reason, besides prescribing the fixed principles of the understanding, without which objectivity is not possible, deals with the empirical according to its own principles, in such a way that the mind both 'adjusts itself to nature' and yet regulates its activity by its own ideal of intelligibility. (*Kant*, p. 231)

However, this may be closer to Lindsay's own view of scientific method as progressive and experimental than to Kant's view.

Lindsay gives an appreciative account of Kant's moral theory. He held that Kant was one of the few philosophers whose views took serious account of the goodness of ordinary simple people. He saw two streams in Kant's view of morality: one, the formalist, where the rational will is simply guided by consistency; the other, more profound one, where rational willing is creative and guided by the respect one rational will has for others.

In general, what I think Lindsay found in Kant and assimilated into his own thinking was this view of moral significance as rational willing, along with a view of knowledge as a combination of theoretical and practical elements as in the methods of the sciences. He thought Kant's account needed to be supplemented by a critique of the biological sciences – nearly produced in the *Critique of Judgement* – and of the historical sciences. He accepted the repudiation of speculative metaphysics, while yet finding metaphysical overtones in moral experience. He saw knowledge as essentially fragmentary, but also as guided by reference to standards of completeness and intelligibility it could never in fact satisfy. In Kant these standards were represented by the Regulative Ideals of the Reason. Lindsay wrote not only of these but also of Kant's Things-in-themselves as if they were limiting concepts in our incomplete, but yet ever-growing, understanding of empirical reality. But there is an important difference. Knowledge of the empirical world grows and progresses as directed towards an ideal of complete, systematic explanation, which it can approach but never fully reach. But we get no nearer (or further) in understanding the nature of Things-in-themselves.

Lindsay was on surer ground in claiming to find in Kant a view of philosophy as 'criticism of standards'; of the standard involved in a branch of knowledge achieving 'the sure path of a science'. He tried to say what he meant by this in the last philosophical paper he wrote, 'Philosophy as a Criticism of Standards', a paper written for the meeting of the Scots Philosophical Club in September 1950, but not delivered in person because of illness.[2] Here he showed that his objection to most of recent philosophy was not so much that it was empirical and opposed to speculative metaphysics – Lindsay himself was that. He objected to it because he thought it did not discuss questions which were important in relation to other things we think important. It was because he believed philosophy ought to be able to do this that he saw it as part of a general education, and he thought that contemporary professional philosophy was becoming a specialism that was ceasing to be able to play this role.

He refers, as he so often did, to Socrates' conviction that there were standards of good and bad workmanship in the crafts, and that there should be something analogous to this in morals and politics. What emerged from this conviction, at least in the way Plato developed it, was a set of further convictions.

(1)   That the standards of craftsmanship and of conduct, though analogous, are not the same. The choice between purposes in the good life is not like the choice of effective means to a given end in a craft.

(2)   Standards are grasped, partly at least, by an element of intuitive understanding.

(3)   There is something akin to this vision in mathematics (although Lindsay dissociates himself from the metaphysical implications Plato saw in mathematics).

So Lindsay's final description of philosophy sees it as a criticism of standards – 'criticism' here meaning the articulation of what they are and how they work in different kinds of rational activity. Philosophy must come to appreciate these standards rather than take on itself to judge what they ought to be. Repeatedly in talking about morals, politics, art, kinds of knowledge, he used the term 'operative ideals'. He spoke of these as an empiricist who was not only an empiricist: he believed that a proper understanding of what was going on in rational activities called for reference to standards transcending anything actually achieved or achievable. These standards, as 'operative', really make a difference to the ways activities are pursued. He would have had no use for references to transcendent ideals which make no difference.

I wish, however, that he had gone further into the various kinds of standard. In this last lecture he notes that they are not all of the same kind, but he says very little about the differences in how they operate. So 'standard' is used to cover a number of logically very different conceptions. For instance:

(1) Sometimes it is the notion of an elusive, transcendent ideal, as the Platonic Idea of the Good.

(2) Sometimes this is thought of as an operative reality, as when he refers to the Puritan's belief in 'the Will of God'.

(3) Sometimes it is an examplar, such as he thinks the Sermon on the Mount gives of the Christian ideal of perfection.

(4) Sometimes a 'standard' is said to be an abstraction defining a particular kind of enquiry or practice, such as the 'economic man' in economics, or the 'reasonable man' in law. Here it is like Max Weber's 'ideal type'.

(5   Sometimes 'standards' are said to be methodological principles guiding enquiries, such as the principle of the uniformity of nature. (These would differ from (4), since any scientific enquiry can contain a group of them; they are guiding assumptions, never in fact proved or fully exemplified.)

(6) Sometimes 'standards' mean intuitively absorbed styles of performance, in art or science; they come from studying the practice of a master, but they do not just copy it.

These are some, not necessarily all, of the kinds of thing Lindsay refers to by the word 'standard'. They are obviously very different, both in their logic and their use.[3]

To H.A. Prichard's question 'Does Moral Philosophy rest on a mistake?', he would not have answered with Prichard 'Yes, in so far as it has talked about desire for the Good in a way that suggests morality has *anything whatever* to do with what we desire.' Lindsay thought that this was to accept a simple hedonistic view of all desires as self-seeking, or at any rate as independent of will and reason. Rather, he was interested in how desires can be transformed as we come to love the things we learn to appreciate. One of the places where he made this distinction most persuasively was in the Balliol College Sermon 'Treasure in Heaven' (published in *The Moral Teaching of Jesus*, London, 1937). Here he looked at the teaching about rewards in the Gospels – teaching which Prichardian moralists cannot explain away and can only reject. He says that 'to regard religion as a means of enjoying unchanged desires is to use spirit and mind to exploit, not to explore' (op. cit., p. 57). Rather, the 'reward' may be that in the Christian commitment we may find that our desires get changed, so that we come to love and enjoy things we could not see or appreciate before; and this is epitomized by the phrase 'Treasure in Heaven'. The 'Good' is not that which satisfies whatever desires we happen to have, but that which we come to appreciate in a way which brings together desire, will, and reason. I think Lindsay would have applauded Miss Iris Murdoch's latter-day Platonism, in her Leslie Stephen lecture, *The Sovereignty of Good over Other Concepts*, London, Routledge, 1970.

In the remaking of our desires, morality can be enhanced by religion, though this remaking need not only happen in a religious context. It can also happen in an artistic one. But Lindsay sees it happening pre-eminently through religion, and he sees religious morality as pre-eminently a morality of examples rather than a morality of rules. It is personal and inspirational: he sees it as a work of 'grace', and it is 'grace' rather than the more traditional 'moral argument for theism', which, I think, is the centre of his religious philosophy.

The quality of 'grace' inspires a kind of morality different from the morality of social codes and reciprocal rights and obligations. He finds it in the Sermon on the Mount, which sets forward a morality of unlimited trust and generosity in the context of the call to perfection. This can never be the morality of the give and take, the limited rights and duties, of ordinary social life; still less can it be a morality enforced by sanctions. He wrote about this contrast in *The Two Moralities* (London, Eyre and Spottiswode, 1940).

Lindsay thinks that we need both these kinds of morality. No society can get on without an average morality, some of which is enforceable by law, which fits in with what on the whole people can expect of each other, especially in those social relations which have to be impersonal and indirect. This kind of morality is relative to historical circumstances, to how people live together in different kinds of society at different times. But no social morality of 'my station and its duties' can work without at any rate some people some of the time infusing into it something of the spirit of the morality of grace. They will not always insist on standing on their rights; they will do generous compassionate things which people have no right to demand of them. And this brings an element of spontaneity, adaptability, creativeness, into the morality of rule and custom, of law and contract.

Perhaps we need to distinguish two kinds of 'morality of grace' which Lindsay fuses together. There is the kind which he epitomizes by quoting from Wordsworth,[4]

> That best portion of a good man's life,
> His little, nameless, unremembered acts
> Of kindness and of love,

and there is the heroic, sacrificial morality of the saint. Both, however, are distinguishable from the morality of codes and of reciprocal rights and obligations. Lindsay's point is that this latter can become rigid, censorious, power-seeking, unless something of the creative, imaginative spirit of the former comes into it (one thinks of what can happen when people 'work to rule', or even work too much 'by the clock'). Yet he also insisted that if a society tried to depend only on the personal, spontaneous morality of grace, it would fall into anarchy. He observed that what passes for 'Christian morality' in our society is a watered-down version which is neither a workable contemporary code, nor the spontaneous morality of grace, and it is this hybrid which he thought the young were repudiating. He also thought that when people repudiated ordinary social morality, they were often the more open to the appeal of the heroic morality of grace. This is surely true of a number of the young 'drop-outs' today. Moreover, he had some perceptive things to say, also not without relevance today, about how a self-sacrificial revolutionary morality can turn into an oppressive revolutionary morality. He saw this happening in the Troubles in Ireland in 1921. When people are struggling as underdogs against what seems inhuman and impersonal power, there is spiritual elation in using violence, as they know they are just as likely – perhaps more likely – to be killed as to kill. They see their violence as justified and they can use it fanatically and oppressively and regard this sense of moral exaltation as sufficient evidence of righteousness.

In its sacrificial quality and its sense of an absolute, the heroic revolutionary morality is more analogous to the morality of grace than to ordinary social morality. It degenerates when it loses contact with the morality of justice and mutual rights. In his view of the interplay between 'the two moralities', Lindsay saw the morality of the call of perfection as 'an operative ideal', never fully realized or indeed realizable, but making ordinary workaday morality workable – perhaps bearable – through infusing something of its spirit into it. But since every society needs some enforceable rules, if these rules are not guided by reciprocity and what can reasonably be expected, people may try to make the heroic, sacrificial morality into a matter of rules. Then it will either turn to rigourism or be watered down – or probably both.

That the two kinds of morality need each other if they are not to degenerate was, I think, the main thing that Lindsay had to say about morals. It was a theme to which he constantly turned. It is also a theme in his political philosophy. Politics belongs to the side of life where the public social morality, particularly in its legal aspects, enters more obviously than does the morality of grace. But Lindsay was concerned to show that the morality of grace also entered into the 'operative ideal' of at any rate a democratic form of society.

He set out his democratic faith over many years in his lecture course on 'The Theory of the Modern State', and some, though not all, of what he had to say about it was published in *The Modern Democratic State* (Oxford, Oxford University Press, 1943) and in the little book *Essentials of Democracy* (Oxford, 1930). It combined a strong view of the need for constitutional and juridical procedures with a strong belief in the worth of every individual, and of the potential contributions which ordinary individuals could make to public life. He saw the roots of modern democracy in the philosophy of Rousseau, and also in the English Puritan revolution of the seventeenth century. He claimed that the Puritan congregations of England, Scotland and New England worked on a conviction of the worth of each member before God, and of the possibility that each member could contribute to the formation of a common mind. When decisions had to be taken, all alike were ready to wait upon 'the will of God', which was not to be identified with what any individual, particularly a dominant individual, happened to want. He may have idealized the extent to which the seventeenth-century Puritan congregations went in for free and tolerant discussion, directed towards a common mind under the will of God. One suspects that the rule of the saints did not always work out like this, though Roger Williams' Quaker congregations and some of the Separatist sects may have come somewhere near it. But Lindsay was surely right in seeing Puritan theology and practice as a factor in the development of British, as distinct from Continental, democracy. No doubt the local Free Churches as schools of democratic leadership belong more to the history of the nineteenth century than the seventeenth. But the seventeenth-century Puritans held a religious conviction about equality, and Lindsay saw this as one ingredient in democratic faith.

This faith in equality, Lindsay distinguished from the secular individualism which looks on people as distinct units (a view which he connected in particular with Hobbes but also detected in the Benthamites). It goes with people being members of a community in which each should feel he counts, to which he can make his contribution. Here Lindsay's mentor was Rousseau, as much as the Puritan divines. And just as the Puritans had seen their associations as working not just for their own power and purposes, but for the 'will of God' – a transcendent ideal – so too Lindsay thought that Rousseau's conception of the General Will, as a *standard* of right and reasonable group decisions, brought in a reference to a transcendent ideal, and prevented the General Will from simply being a glorification of the power of the majority, or even of the unanimous opinion of a group as such. He was convinced that unless democracy contained some transcendent reference beyond the interests and power of the group itself, it would degenerate into majority tyranny, or be manipulated by power-seeking politicians, and lose its creative exploratory character. Nevertheless, he did think that loyalty to democratic procedures almost had a 'will of God' quality about it, not because *vox populi* was *vox dei* – far from it – but because this was a moral condition for the possibility of democratic life. He used to tell a story of a Scottish minister who had vehemently opposed something in the Synod. When nevertheless this went through by a majority vote, the minister was found working wholeheartedly for it. 'But,' they said 'you thought it was wrong and foolish.' 'I still think it is wrong and I still think it is foolish, but I have come to see that it is the will of God.' There spoke the constitutional democrat.

But Lindsay not only believed in the importance of constitutional procedures. He also believed in the importance of widespread discussion and concern in public questions. Here he saw the role of a multiplicity of free associations within the total community. He was not a political pluralist, in that he thought that the State had a unique directing role (though not necessarily a superior moral authority). But he was a pluralist in that he believed in the importance of free associations within the community. These, he thought, could best play a role in public life if they were not specifically political (though of course, he saw the need for some specifically political organizations, and was himself a member of the Labour Party). There need to be associations with interests and purposes of their own, whose members are prepared, when occasion arises, to feel a 'concern' for problems in the wider community in a public-spirited way. An existing draft chapter (all that can be found of what was presumably meant to go into the unwritten second volume of *The Modern Democratic State*) discusses the question of a ruling class in a democracy. It differs from most 'elitist' literature in not seeing this as a distinct (though not necessarily class) section of the population – still less as made up of professional politicians – but as potentially drawn from any part of the community, where people have the will and interest, and are prepared to give the time, to take part in political and public affairs. They can thus sometimes be in and sometimes out of politics. Also the multifarious associations of non-political life provide training grounds where people learn to work the procedures of democratic decision and practice.

Possibly Lindsay overestimated the influence, and indeed the public-spirited disinterestedness, of non-political small groups. He did not take a long look at the 'iron law of oligarchy', the tendency of any group to get run by a self-perpetuating clique, and the need to counteract this. Nor did he look at the extent to which groups are likely, quite non-deliberately, to give special weight to their own interests in talking about the public interest. His enthusiasm for the unselfish devotion of particular small groups could carry him away into speaking as though what they were doing could count for more than in some circumstances it possibly could. An example was his conviction about the importance of the experiment in which some unemployed clubs in Lincoln undertook imaginative unpaid pieces of social service in the 1930s under the guidance of his friend Alice Cameron. In some BBC broadcasts 'I Believe in Democracy' on democracy to Europe in May and June 1940, he had prepared an address for 17 June in which he intended to talk about how democracies could deal with unemployment, and he refers to this work (published in Japan by Asahi Press). Now whatever the problems of democracy in June 1940, how to use leisure in unemployment was not one of them; and in the event, on the news of France's surrender, Lindsay substituted a moving address on democracy fighting for its life; we may survive this attack, he says 'but if not' – and here is the text of the talk, taken from the Book of Daniel – '*but if not*, know, O King, that we will not serve thy gods, nor worship the golden image which thou hast set up'. He calls attention to how the unforeseen success of Dunkirk had come not through some spectacular miracle, but through the courage and resourcefulness and steadiness of the ordinary citizen soldiers of democracy – and, he might have added, of the civilian navigators of small boats.

So his democratic faith rested on his belief in the qualities of ordinary men and women. And these were qualities which depended for their creativeness on the interplay between the 'two moralities': social morality and the morality of grace, an interplay which comes out in generosity and compassion shown by ordinary people, as well as in the sacrificial heroism of the saints.

The general will is a standard, an 'operative ideal', which should guide legislation, and which to some extent does guide it in a practising democracy; and we see that the State has a special role as the legislative and administrative institution within the community. This is where he parted company with pluralists such as Harold Laski; he discussed this point with Laski in an Aristotelian Society Symposium in 1928.[5] In this discussion Lindsay drew on what is perhaps the clearest, best-argued paper he ever wrote, the paper on 'Sovereignty' given to the Aristotelian Society in 1924.[6] Here he started from criticizing the Austinian doctrine of Sovereignty, by which Law is seen as a command, and the political distinction as being between a sovereign who commands and subjects who obey. He shows that the impossibility of finding a concrete 'determinate superior' in a democratic or indeed constitutional state means that here the Austinian theory cannot fit the facts. Nevertheless, just to make 'Sovereignty' a matter of seeing what group at any given time happens to have most political power (Laski's view) will not do either. It confuses a question of the political sociology of power with the juristic question of how to determine what rules in the community shall be rules of law. Constitutional government means accepting a principle which decides this by agreed procedures. So the juristic theory of sovereignty points not to a 'determinate human superior' issuing commands, but to a definite principle by which what is law can be determined. This bears an affinity to Kelsen's view of the nature of a legal system which H.L.A. Hart developed further in *The Concept of Law* (Oxford, 1961). A legal system has a 'rule of recognition' which enables other rules to be identified as rules of the system. Professor Hart told me in conversation that he agrees that his view, and Kelsen's, on this defining characteristic of a legal system is there in principle, independently stated, in Lindsay's 1924 paper. Lindsay's view of Sovereignty as a matter of seeing the final word on a legislative decision as depending on the constitution may be relevant to contemporary considerations of Parliamentary Sovereignty and our membership of the European Union. Lindsay spoke in terms of the unitary sovereignty of the nation state. But the final word may not have to rest with the same body for all purposes; different powers for certain purposes may rest with different bodies. Yet Lindsay would surely say (and rightly) that any division of powers (as distinct from 'power') must be a constitutional matter; and the constitution must determine where each of the powers ultimately lies.

Lindsay's view of sovereignty of the constitution is a juridical theory, and not a theory of power. It is consistent with actual power being widely dispersed, and not all concentrated in government, though he also believed that a government should command sufficient force, and be prepared to use it to defend decisions constitutionally arrived at. But this does not mean that there are no other centres of power at any given time, and still less does it mean that the main political distinction is between those who command and those who obey. The juridical democratic state operates as a central co-ordinating institution within a community where a multitude of different kinds of associations also have power and powers for their own purposes.

In seeing these associations as sources of public spirit, Lindsay may have underestimated the pull of self-interest. This was why Rousseau objected to particular associations, not seeing they were also potentially fruitful in the life of the community. Rousseau wanted to run all sides of its life through a single monolithic group. Hence his view by itself leads either to the glorification of the very small community, or to the perversions of 'totalitarian democracy'. Lindsay saw that a view fitted to the former could not deal with the political problems of mass societies; and he looked for the safeguard against the latter in strong constitutional government within a pluralistic community of non-political associations, whose members were prepared to have political views and exercise public spirit.

Lindsay proposed to discuss the international implications of his views on democratic life and leadership in the second volume of *The Modern Democratic State*, but this never got written. How he might have approached this on the economic side is suggested by what he says about 'economic determinism' in his book *Karl Marx's Capital* (given originally as WEA (Workers' Educational Association) lectures in Glasgow in the early 1920s) (London and New York, Oxford University Press, 1925). He shows that 'economic determinism' need not imply a denial of individual free will. It is a structural sociological point about how people's uncoordinated actions can add up on a large scale to results which no one likes and no one intended.

He then speaks of the need to bring these under control through common purposes co-operatively pursued. Yes indeed; but had he a strong enough sense of the complexity of economic forces in modern international society, and our bounded rationality in understanding and controlling them? A tough-minded contemporary might say[7] that with this optimistic faith in the power of a common purpose, Lindsay's political philosophy is still too 'idealist'. He did indeed have a much stronger appreciation than either Green or Bosanquet of the conflicts within an industrial society, and so for the need for industrial and not only political democracy, and for the need for experts and political leadership. What he did was to carry forward the constructive side of the idealist theory of the State, in the liberal sense in which Green and Bosanquet had expressed it, seeing the State as the protector of right, providing a secure framework for non-political activities within a lively community. What he meant by 'common purpose' was a co-ordinated effort to uphold and further the life of the community in this sense.

He saw more clearly than either Green or Bosanquet that non-political groupings, following their own purposes, could play back onto political life by encouraging public-spirited action when and where particular social needs arose. This was in fact something to which he dedicated his own life within the University. He had a clearer view than either Green or Bosanquet of the juridical and administrative sides of the modern state, and an empirical acquaintance with how things could be worked politically which some people thought was almost Machiavellian. If this was so, it was off-set by a genuine sense of the pull of 'operative ideals', which led him to respect people's moral convictions even when he disagreed with them.

Much of his life was that of an administrator; but an administrator who was also a political philosopher, and a political philosopher who had behind him a theory of knowledge. This made him see knowledge as starting from experimental empirical action, and as coming back to it; and empirical knowledge so gained as exploratory and fragmentary within a world which was vast, mysterious and largely unknown. Empirical knowledge and action could be guided by transcendent ideals. Among these ideals, that which had the most creative effect on his own thinking was the Christian ideal of perfection, seen as a source inspiring compassion, love, generosity. More than once towards the end of his life he wrote that what the world needed was 'the scientific mind in the service of the merciful heart', and once added 'the reverential heart'. His operative ideals were Platonic, Kantian, Christian; above all, Christian. But the influence of Bergson's view of how the simplest as well as the most complex forms of knowledge involve free creative activity should not be underestimated.

Lindsay was not a 'philosophers' philosopher'. Most professional philosophy among his contemporaries, and still more as it has since developed in universities in English-speaking countries, calls for standards of logical rigour and detailed analytic discussion for which he had little interest or inclination. But what he gave me was not just preaching. It was a way of thinking conveyed more through lectures than in books and articles, and it is no accident that many of his books grew out of lectures. The audiences at his lectures, especially those on Plato's *Republic* and 'The Theory of the Modern State', filled Balliol hall over a generation. They came from many backgrounds and many countries, and are now scattered widely over the world in many walks of life. They listened to a man who took a philosophical stance and drew on the resources of a rich mind to talk about moral and political questions in ways which affected how many of them would go on thinking of them. This kind of lecture is not a present style, and indeed Lindsay may have been its last great representative. It was the style of a man thinking aloud about things he believed mattered, often bringing them to life in the good story, the humble incident, the passage from a poem or a novel. It was the style of a man who believed that intellectual and practical concerns must be brought together, and who tried to bring them together in his own mind.

4

Philosophy Among the
South Wales Miners

The General Strike of 1926 came in the middle of my time at Oxford. A number of undergraduates went off to do manual work. For instance, one went to Paddington Station and was told to oil the points. Some days later a message came from Bristol: 'Send more oil.' I did not want to go strike-breaking, and in any case women under-graduates were not allowed to go away. Some of us collected round Lindsay, who was supporting a proposal of the then Archbishop of Canterbury, that the Government and strikers should hold talks. We went out on bicycles collecting signatures for this, and were getting well going when the General Strike was called off. One evening of that week I listened to a talk in support of the miners by R.H. Tawney. Tawney combined superb wit with cutting invective and a Christian fire in his belly.

That speech gave me the nearest thing I have had to a conversion experience, leading me to be seriously concerned about political matters. That summer vacation I spent some time in a mining district in North Staffordshire (the miners were still out) and also took part in the WEA Summer School at Balliol where I did some tutoring and helped organize the social side. I did this in July for several years. On one occasion the World's YMCA (of which the average age appeared to be about 60) was having a conference in another part of Balliol, and they asked whether anyone in the WEA school could take some of their overseas members round colleges and I volunteered. One man with a black beard and piercing eyes asked me what I did. When I said I was a philosophy student, he said so was he, and he was a Russian. I said I had just been reading a book by a Russian philoso-pher, Berdyaev. I wondered whether he knew him. We were speaking in French, and he exclaimed 'Certainement je le connais. Moi je suis Berdyaev'. Berdyaev had been Professor of Philosophy in

Moscow under the Soviets, but had come to think of human destiny in terms of a mystical spiritual freedom, and had gone into exile.

After I went down I joined two Quakers, William and Emma Noble, at Maesynhaf Settlement in the mining district of the Rhondda Valley of South Wales. There was about 80 per cent unemployment; the dole was meagre and the poverty was such as is not known nowadays. The Settlement was both doing educational work and promoting various kinds of self-help. My part consisted in running WEA classes. Most of the members of those classes were unemployed miners, and some of them had come over from former classes held by the National Council of Labour Colleges, a Marxist organisation which had lately gone bankrupt. So our classes had a strong Marxist element besides people whose roots were still in the Chapel. This meant that there was always scope for vigorous arguments, very often on morals, economics and politics. I can see now that I took an over-personalised view of Marxist moral philosophy: the corrective came later in the 1930s, when I had to come more closely to terms with Marxism, and I shall try to say something about this in that context. My classes were largely based on Plato's *Republic*. I might not do them like this now, but my Oxford background with Lindsay had made me think that a way into philosophy was through Plato's *Republic*. And indeed there are few books which produce more talking points, always good for argument. A young man in one of my classes was called George Thomas. He was to become Speaker of the House of Commons, and many years later he invited me to visit him at Westminster. One of these occasions was a dinner in the Speaker's House. After dinner George said something about each guest at the table so as to show us what his link with us was. When he came to me, he said, 'Dorothy, when she went down from Oxford, came to us in the Rhondda Valley. She brought us a box of books, and I looked after the box of books.'

My colleague in this venture was Henry Brooke, who had also recently gone down from Oxford. I came to appreciate Henry's real goodness, generally hidden by his stuffed-shirt image when he was Home Secretary. He said that the experience in the Rhondda made him a Conservative. Faced with the rhetorical ebullience of our Welsh miner students, he said 'What this valley needs is discipline.' He never looked back.

My own experience in those classes, however, did not lead me into politics, but made me more convinced that I must try to do philosophy, though I did not then envisage doing it as a university teacher. I read Whitehead's *Science and the Modern World*, which had come out in 1926. This brought me back to central questions about the nature of things. I still think that *Science and the Modern World* was an inspired book; it got overlaid by the complexities of Whitehead's later work. I was attracted by his suggestion of an enlarged philosophy of organism, though I could not properly see what this was. On a visit to Oxford from South Wales, I saw my former tutor, Charles Morris, at Balliol and he urged me to go to America and study with Whitehead. I put in for a Commonwealth (later called a Harkness) Fellowship and was called for interview. I was asked why I wanted to study with Whitehead, and when I said 'Because I can't understand him', they laughed. But they must have thought it was a good enough reason, as I got the Fellowship.

Before passing on to what I made of Whitehead there is, however, one incident I would like to record from my times in South Wales when I went back for another winter after my return from the States. I went to Oxford for a weekend, and looked in on the Lindsays. It was about 12 o'clock on a Saturday and I found Mrs Lindsay desperately telephoning for a taxi to go to the station to meet Gandhi, who was about to arrive for a private weekend conference in the Master's Lodgings about possible constitutional developments for India. Nowadays no doubt secretaries and security men would be on the job. Then it was left for Mrs Lindsay to get a taxi and none seemed to be available. I shyly said I had a car outside, and should I go? The offer was accepted. At the station I introduced myself to the station master and said I had come to meet Mr Gandhi. My car was one of the old Baby Austins – open with a hard back seat. An enormous detective got into the seat beside me and Gandhi, wrapped in his homespun cloth, perched on the seat behind. It was the midday Saturday train from London and there were a number of cars meeting it. These were all held back while my Baby Austin with Gandhi and the detective on board sailed down the ramp. Gandhi talked affably over my shoulder, but I thought I had better concentrate on the traffic, and I slipped away after depositing him at the Master's Lodgings. When I got back to South Wales and told members of my classes that I had been driving Gandhi, they were thrilled; one of them even asked to touch the car. Gandhi was a hero to the British working class at that time, in spite of the fact that his non-cooperation campaign was exacerbating unemployment.

5

A.N. Whitehead
in Cambridge, Mass.

I took up my Commonwealth Fellowship at Radcliffe College, Cambridge, Mass. in 1928. Radcliffe was in close proximity to Harvard College. There was a form of association, but emphatically not integration as there is now. Radcliffe degrees were not Harvard degrees, and, while women could take part in graduate seminars, Radcliffe students were not allowed to attend undergraduate lectures in Harvard. In the case of Whitehead's lectures this was an advantage as far as I was concerned. In Harvard Whitehead lectured to a class of about 70. In Radcliffe there were about eight of us, and so we had genuine personal contact. I also saw a good deal of Whitehead and his wife. I think they liked having an English girl to talk to who had something of their own background and with whom they could share reflections (generally but not universally favourable) about the ways of American Society. They much appreciated the zest for ideas and were totally free from the intellectual snobbery of some British scholars. They had met this zest on their arrival to take up the chair, when their boat landed in Boston and a customs officer came to examine their luggage spread on the quayside. He asked what was in one box, and when he was told 'Books' demanded that it should be opened. The top book was on the Principle of Relativity, on which he said 'I always wanted to understand this', and got Whitehead to give him a lecture sitting on a trunk. On the debit side the Whiteheads were distressed by what even then was the sexual promiscuity among students. Mrs Whitehead told me never to say I had had experience, as that could mean only one thing.

Whitehead held a graduate seminar in his apartment on Fridays from 7.30 to 9.30. Members gave papers on matters of their choice, so these seminars were not directly concerned with Whitehead's own philosophy, though indirectly this would come out in his wide-ranging comments on the papers. Whitehead has been likened in his appearance to a benign Mr Pickwick. But when he began to talk, the talk was penetrating and at times epigrammatic. Some of these remarks have been recorded by A.H. Johnson in *The Wit and Wisdom of Alfred North Whitehead* (Boston, Beacon Press, 1947). Johnson was a close pupil; the book contains an excellent introduction. After the seminar Mrs Whitehead brought in refreshments – cakes and hot chocolate, but no alcohol. The Whiteheads themselves were fond of wine, but these were the days of Prohibition, and they made it a matter of principle that as visiting residents they ought to keep the law. (This surprised some of their colleagues.) There was good general conversation as well as open-ended philosophical discussion. The Whiteheads held open-house to graduate students (also wives and fiancées) on Sunday evenings when there would be more general conversation and informed intellectual discussion. This kind of 'at home' was a practice brought from the old world to the new which surprised Whitehead's Harvard colleagues. One frequent participant was the French philosopher Etienne Gilson, then a visiting scholar. I had the privilege of attending his seminar on St Thomas Aquinas, my initiation into this important philosophy. It was a notable exercise; Gilson dismissed us on one occasion with the pronouncement 'God, you must remember, is *unique*' (pronounced 'eunuch'). We found pleasure in repeating this to each other. Both Whitehead and his wife were notable conversationalists. A number of conversations were recorded and published by Lucien Price in *Dialogues of Alfred North Whitehead* (1954). These recall reflections of the kind I remember, but the book comes from a later time, when Whitehead was more apt to hold forth. But he certainly would not have wanted people to turn him into a sage. More importantly, Lucien Price was a Classical Arts man, and he brought out the side of Whitehead which responded to those interests. There is little to suggest that he was a philosopher of science. That side should be borne in mind in interpreting his philosophy. I myself failed to give it enough weight in the book *Whitehead's Philosophy of Organism* (1932) which arose out of some lectures I was asked to give in Oxford on my return. The book was taken up as an introduction to Whitehead's philosophy; it was marked by youthful enthusiasm and exegetic inadequacy, and I would discourage people from reading it now (or, if they do so, I would encourage them to read the Preface to the Second Edition in which I tried to say something to put the record straight). The book drew on one of Whitehead's rare letters, and as his criticisms are also a statement of his own position, I quote it:

(1) You seem to me at various points to forget my doctrine of 'immanence' which governs the whole treatment of objectification. Thus at times you write as tho' the connection between past and present is merely that of a transfer of *character*. Then there arises [sic] all the perplexities of 'correspondence' in epistemology, of causality, and of memory. The doctrine of *immanence* is fundamental.

(2) You neglect the fundamental character of subjective form. The subject-object relation is the emotional life of the subject derived from the objects and directed towards them. But the drive towards self-formation is in the subjective form. The continuity in nature is a continuity of subjective form. Cf. in the Index under 'Conformal feelings' and 'Subjective form.' Remember that consciousness is *not* the fundamental basis of experience – so that the subject-object relation is not fundamentally subject-conscious-of-object.

(3) You sometimes write as if my doctrine of sense-perception were fundamental. For P. and R., sense-perception is a highly sophisticated outcome of the higher phases of experience – and *for this reason* very prominent in consciousness – cf. P. and R., Part IV, last chapter, also in Index under *'Sense perception'* or *'Presentational Immediacy.'*

But do not let these remarks give you the impression that I am not pleased with the book – quite the contrary. I have read it with profit and appreciation.

Whitehead himself is reported to have said that I made him 'too Platonic'. That he was a kind of latter-day Platonist was a general impression at the time, owing, no doubt, to the role given in *Process and Reality* to 'eternal objects', which looked like Platonic ideas. The writer of his obituary in *The Times* called him 'the last and greatest of the Cambridge Platonists'. Whitehead had given the Gifford Lectures in Edinburgh in 1928, and when I was in his classes in 1929 he was turning them into *Process and Reality*. He believed that he could sometimes say what he wanted better in verbal exposition than when writing, so sometimes when he came to a hard passage he would signal to me to get it down *verbatim* and afterwards asked for my notes. I recognize some of these passages in *Process and Reality*; I take no responsibility except as an amanuensis. So the later Whitehead was the Whitehead I knew. I culpably failed to give proper attention to the Whitehead who worked with Russell in *Principia Mathematica* or on the philosophy of science in the books of the middle period.

There are seminal ideas in these books which became overlaid by the complexities of *Process and Reality* with its often obfuscating terminology. One interpreter of Whitehead who did something to trace these ideas was Victor Lowe in *Understanding Whitehead* (Baltimore, Johns Hopkins Press, 1962), and in the two volumes of his biography, *A.N. Whitehead: The Man and his Work* (Johns Hopkins, 1985 and 1990). I would draw attention particularly to chapters 5 and 6 in Volume II on the philosophy of natural science in the middle period. These chapters were contributed by Leemon B. McHenry, since Lowe was unable to finish the second volume owing to failing health. Also books by Wolfe Mays, *The Philosophy of Whitehead* (Allen and Unwin, London, 1959) and Whitehead's *Essays in Science and Metaphysics* (New York, 1947) bring out how his metaphysics was affected by the logic of propositional functions. Mays quotes Whitehead's saying in his Forward to Quine's *System of Logistic* 'The reformation of Logic has an essential reference to Metaphysics. For Logic prescribes the shapes of Metaphysical Thought.' This line of thought is also profitably taken up by James Bradley in some as yet unpublished articles and in the entry on Whitehead which he has contributed to the forthcoming Routledge Encyclopedia of Philosophy. He most interestingly compares Whitehead's approach to that of Intuitionist mathematicians such as Brouwer. Serious students should look out for these articles.

Presenting Whitehead as a philosopher of science might help to bring some of his thought back to the attention of mainline analytic philosophers. At present the virtual concentration on the metaphysics of *Process and Reality* among 'process philosophers' in America has led to these Whiteheadians constructing a world of their own with little or no communication with other kinds of philosophers. This is largely, though not entirely, true of the contributors to *Process Studies*, and is very true of the school of Whitehead studies at Claremont, California. They have tended to build Whitehead up into a guru. There is also a tendency to concentrate on religious implications of his views and in so doing to try to bring them into line with more traditional Christian views. I would make exceptions here of Professor John Cobb, who has a critically independent approach, and also of Professor Charles Hartshorne who worked out his philosophy of religion independently of Whitehead's, though he acknowledges affinities with it. I cannot myself go along with some of Hartshorne's views, but I find them impressive.

There is now a certain amount of interest in Whitehead on the continent of Europe, notably in Germany. There have been two seminar-conferences, one in Bonn and one in Bad Homberg near Frankfurt, and the proceedings of these (published by Verlag Karl Alber, Freiburg/Munich), *Whitehead und der Prozessbegriff* (1984) and *Whitehead's Metaphysick der Creativität* (1986) contain a wide range of contributions. The conferences were in German and English, the Proceedings of the former conference contain abstracts in English of the German papers and in German of the English ones. The Proceedings of the second are almost entirely in German but there is an English version edited by F. Rapp and R. Wiehl, *Whitehead's Metaphysics of Creativity* (Albany, State University of New York Press, 1990). Anyone interested in totally non-sectarian discussions of Whitehead's philosophy could well consult these volumes.

In the rest of this chapter I shall not try to give a synopsis of Whitehead's philosophy, even if I could. I shall signal some ideas which I have found profitable to pursue, others where I have seen trouble ahead. I am aware that Whitehead's manner of presentation is very different from what would be expected in most Anglo-American philosophy. More argument would be called for and more elucidation; more replies to possible objections. Broadly, I shall be trying to indicate some of the clues which I have tried to follow when discussing him with my contemporaries.

I now find my main clue in the way in which Whitehead combined a concern for logico-mathematical schemes with an interest in the richly complex world we experience. He wanted to show how the former could be exemplified in the latter, and indeed could be derived from it by processes of abstraction. But the abstractions must not be treated as though they were the realities; to do so was to commit what he called 'The Fallacy of Misplaced Concreteness'. Russell noted these two sides in his *Portraits from Memory* (London, Allen and Unwin, 1956). '[Whitehead] said to me once "you think the world is what it looks like in fair weather at noon-day. I think it is like what it seems like in the early morning when one first wakes from deep sleep". I thought his remark was horrid, but could not see how to prove that my bias was better than his. At last he showed me how to apply the techniques of mathematical logic to his higgledy-piggledy world and dress it up in Sunday clothes that a mathematician could view without being shocked' (op. cit., p. 41).

One instance is given in the Method of Extensive Abstraction. In experience we never find points and instants without extension. But we do experience areas extending over other areas and temporal occurrences extending over other temporal occurrences. We can imagine these extensions as diminishing on a regular scale.

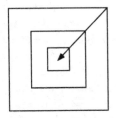

The point or the instant is defined as the route of approximation – it does not exist at the ideal limit of the approximation, since no actual extensionless point or instant can be experienced. What we can experience are areas diminishing in extension. Yet the exactness in a route of diminishing extensions shown in the Method of Extensive Abstraction is a piece of topology and is surely a very extreme idealization of anything that could be experienced in perception. Whitehead acknowledged this at times when he spoke of the exactness as a 'fake'. Nevertheless, his aim was to find patterns of relatedness which could be exemplified in different kinds of experience. This, I think, underlay his great interest in drawing analogies, including analogies between historical periods or between different societies. Some of these are illuminating and some may seem far-fetched; they are motivated, I think, by the desire to find concrete exemplifications of abstract generalities. He put this by saying 'the procedure of rationalism is the discussion of analogy. The limitation of rationalism is the inescapable diversity' (*Modes of Thought*, Cambridge, 1938, p. 134).

Victor Lowe refers to an occasion on which John Dewey asked Whitehead to choose between a mathematical-formal interpretation of his method in philosophy and a genetic-functional one. 'Whitehead of course declined to choose, and said the real problem for philosophers was the fusion of these two ways of looking at first principles.'[1] He was trying to hold together a way of looking on the world as made up of dynamic processes in interconnections and as exhibiting structures which could be exhibited in mathematical and logical form. So he looked for exemplifications of some pattern of relations in different fields of experience, often describing them by analogies. But there seems to be a large gap between the formal scheme and the concrete actualities in which he claims to find the similarities in the relationships formulated abstractly in these schemes.

In Whitehead's earlier work, the most fundamental relation was extensive connection – the world as composed of events extending over and being extended over by other events. What he called the 'Extensive Continuum' was more basic than the Space-Time continuum. Spatio-temporal relations between events were to be abstracted from their extensive connections as successive, overlapping, or congruent. Units in extensive connections are events, and events have characters, for example 'whiteness'. The characters are called, not I think very happily, 'objects', and answer to what in other philosophies could be called 'universals'. In his later work these were called 'eternal objects', leading, as I have said, to a way of interpreting him as a latter-day Platonist. Rather, he was closer to Aristotle's view of *universalia in rebus*, or, as he put it, of 'the forms in the facts'. But he also claims that 'in the place of the Aristotelian notion of the procession of forms [physics] has substituted the notion of the forms of process' (*Modes of Thought*, p. 192). Indeed, this change did not have to wait for the 'new physics' if this means post-nineteenth-century physics. From the seventeenth century on, instead of a world of things seeking to realize their essential natures, we have a world of energy displaying mathematical laws. Nature should be seen as patterns of interrelated activities passing from one state to another. 'Passing' means that the notion of *process* becomes crucial. Whitehead seems to have realized this after he had written an enquiry concerning *The Principles of Natural Knowledge* (Cambridge, 1919), and in the second edition of this book (1927) he added an extremely important note, that

> the book is dominated by the idea that the relation of extension has a unique pre-eminence and that everything can be got out of it ... But the true doctrine that 'process' is the fundamental idea, was not in my mind with sufficient emphasis. Extension is derivative from process, and is required by it. (op. cit., p. 202)

We still have extensive connection, a world of events extending over other events, but these are seen as in transition. Our primary intuition of nature is that of 'passage', of 'something going on' (*The Concept of Nature*, Cambridge, 1920). It is a process, but one which is not simply a succession of events. It is a process of continual formation, transformation, breaking, reforming of patterns of events, and so 'the passage of nature [which] is only another name for the creative force of existence' (op. cit., p. 73).

The introduction of the notion of creativity seems to require that the constituent parts of nature should have, so to speak, more flesh and blood on them than is given in the notion of events extending over other events. In *Science and the Modern World* (Cambridge, 1926), the book which came out of his Lowell Lectures at Harvard in 1925, he begins to speak of *organisms*. This was where I came in and I hoped that he was going to work out a general theory of organism which might bridge the physical and biological sciences. I do not think this ever quite happened, but I still think *Science and the Modern World* was an inspired book and contains suggestions which we can see further developed in his *Adventures of Ideas* (1933) and *Modes of Thought*. When people ask me what they should read of Whitehead's I sometimes suggest they should go from *Science and the Modern World* to *Adventures of Ideas*, skipping the elaborate complexities of *Process and Reality*. These may in fact obscure rather than throw light on the main features.

Some reviewer of *Science and the Modern World* said that it seemed as though it had been written by Dr Jekyll and Mr Hyde, and when one of them began a chapter you never knew which one would finish it. There are parts which are eminently readable, when Whitehead is giving his reflections on the history of European Science and his reasons for thinking that the static materialism, which had sometimes been associated with it, had now had its day. Then there are parts which are extremely difficult and presented with very little in the way of explanation. Readers should not be deterred if they cannot follow these. But they can be on the lookout for certain general ideas which Dr Jekyll and Mr Hyde hold in common. A central notion is that of a 'primary organism'; this is not an elementary living thing, but a unification of the whole of nature in a perspective from a particular centre, which is the situation of what is called a 'percipient' or 'co-gredient' event. This need not be a conscious percipient any more than the observer in Special Relativity need be. It is a centre from which a structured ordering of the rest of the world is developed. But there is more to the primary organism that internal relatedness of events from a centre. Whitehead speaks of 'the emergence of some particular pattern as grasped in the unity of a real event' (*Science and the Modern World*, Cambridge, 1926, p. 146). 'Grasped' is a word suggesting activity, and these primary organisms are being thought of as the centre of active relations to other such centres throughout nature. These active relations are called 'prehensions'. A prehension is the grasping of one thing by another, like a monkey taking hold of a branch with its prehensile tail. It need not be conscious – grasping something in conscious awareness would be 'apprehension'.

It seems bizarre to think of events as active, and not simply as occurring, and in his later philosophy Whitehead calls the final constituents of his world not 'events' but 'actual entities'. An actual entity is called a 'concrescence of prehensions', something which grows together and develops itself out of its active relations to the others in its world. I find this a helpful notion; indeed I can think of myself as a 'concrescence of prehensions' better than I can in terms of most views of the self, and this book might be taken as illustrating it in the process of my self-formation as a philosopher. There are difficulties however over Whitehead's view of prehensions, in that any larger-scale organism is described as a 'society' made up of routes of actual entities. Whitehead spoke of a 'cell' theory, and of all larger-scale organisms, and indeed what we should normally call physical objects, as 'societies composed of large numbers of routes of these cell like actual entities'. I also find a difficulty over causation in this idea of societies of actual entities prehending each other, and occurring in routes, where actual entities perish and are succeeded by others. Each several entity perishes and when it has perished, some aspects of it are 'prehended' and incorporated into the developing nature of other actual entities, either as its successors or as in its environment. Thus a prehension is a *picking up* of something now dead and gone rather than a *passing on* of something from the past into the present. Insofar as the notion of prehension contains Whitehead's view of causal efficacy, this suggests a backward causation and there is also a difficulty over interaction. To go into my reasons for finding this view unsatisfactory would be a longer story than can be told here.[2] I can only call attention to my disquiet. This does not, however, prevent my thinking that the notion of a concrescence of prehensions is a useful one.

It was also found useful by C.H. Waddington, who was foremost among philosophically minded biologists in acknowledging a debt to Whitehead. He summarized this by saying 'As far as scientific practice is concerned the lessons to be learned from Whitehead were not so much derived from his discussions of experiences, but rather by his replacement of "things" by processes which have an individual character which depends on the concrescence into a unity with very many relations with other processes.'[3]

Whitehead was to call his later work 'the Philosophy of Organism', and here the notion of organism has gone beyond that of the primary organism of *Science and the Modern World*, which was a unification of events throughout nature in a perspective from a central event. The unification now becomes a process of self-formation. Whitehead expounded his view of a pluralistic system of these processes of self-formation, with their interrelations and also their inner subjective aspects, in his Gifford Lectures in Edinburgh in 1928. These set out a metaphysical system, summarily presented at the beginning under eight categories of existence, 27 categories of explanation, and nine categoreal (*sic*) obligations. I have been told that the first lecture drew a huge audience, whereas the final one consisted of one or two professors, notably his faithful admirer Professor Kemp Smith. A number of Whitehead's books were first presented as lectures; very little is given by way of explanation, and even as books they require several readings. The manner is almost entirely expository; there is little engagement with the views of contemporaries. He draws on philosophers of the past, but generally in order to suggest analogies with something he wants to say, for instance in his quoting of Locke's phrase about time as 'a perpetual perishing'. He told us in one of his lectures that we should never take his remarks on the history of philosophy as intended to be critically accurate.

The Gifford Lectures were developed in *Process and Reality*, and Whitehead called this an essay in cosmology. I remember him saying 'Write on my tombstone "He tried to form a cosmology".' He meant by a cosmology a general view of the nature of the universe (in the widest sense of the term – not just our universe after, say, the Big Bang) throughout cosmic history, and as studied by the sciences. This was different from Metaphysics which was an attempt to formulate the general nature of anything that could exist in any possible world, and this, he held, would be a single uniform system of concepts. (Any actual metaphysical essay would only be an attempt to imagine what this might be, so any actual formulation would be corrigible.) A cosmology need not attempt to reach a unique set of concepts. Whitehead held that there could be 'cosmic epochs' between which even the Laws of Nature might undergo changes. This was a highly unusual view, but I believe that some contemporary cosmologists are prepared to entertain the possibility that even some physical constants might change over the vast aeons of cosmic evolution. For Whitehead Laws of Nature were not a grid imposed on things; they were generalizations of uniformities in the ways in which things in nature behaved. Over cosmic epochs the behaviour might change on a large scale. (There are still constraints, which I shall come to.)

So even the Laws of Nature are what they are because of generalizations from the ways the constituents of Nature behave, and not the other way around. Whitehead saw this as implied by what he called 'the ontological principle'. This has nothing to do with the Ontological Argument in Natural Theology. It is an assertion that 'the reasons for things are always to be found in the composite nature of definite actual entities'.[4] To think otherwise would be to commit the Fallacy of Misplaced Concreteness. Then what is the composite nature of actual entities? I have noted in Whitehead's late philosophy the ultimate constituents are spoken of as 'actual entities' and not as 'events'. This may be because in this 'philosophy of organism' they are thought of as active and it seems unnatural to speak of events as active. But I am not sure whether this was what Whitehead had in mind, or that he realized explicitly how much of a change this was. The change consisted mainly in insisting that actual entities had an inner subjective aspect besides an outer objective aspect apprehended by others. This inner aspect is experienced in our own emotional life, and on his principle that all actual entities are of the same fundamental kind, something like this, no doubt in a lowly form, is to be found in the inner aspect of everything. So 'the energetic activity considered in physics is the emotional intensity entertained in life'.[5] Whereas the 'primary organisms' of *Science and the Modern World* were events throughout nature unified in token reflexivity to a central event, in *Process and Reality* an organism has subjective feelings and a 'subjective aim' towards its self-development. Whereas in the earlier view, the insistence that there is only one kind of actuality seemed to be leading to a view of biology as being swallowed by a form of Special Relativity physics, in the later view it looks as if physics was being swallowed by a form of psychophysiology. All actual entities have some inner experience; this,

Whitehead insists, is not an Idealist view, since it does not mean that they are dependent on mind, nor need the sentient experience be conscious. Whitehead illustrated this by reference to bodily sensations of which we are only dimly and peripherally aware, and of their importance in sense-perception. He held that in talking of sense-perception philosophers had tended to concentrate too much on clear and distinct visual sensations. I think this is broadly true. The Philosophy building at Harvard had an inscription over the entrance: it was something very high-minded. Whitehead once said to us in a class 'You will have seen that inscription over the door as you came in. I suggest you substitute for it "Meditate on your viscera".' Our bodies are receptors of influences from the outer world, coming as feelings raised into consciousness in perception. Whitehead seems to be fastening on our psycho-physiological embodied experience, and stretching it upward and downward; upward into conscious experiences and downwards into some form of 'feeling' in everything. He repudiated what he called 'vacuous actuality', the notion of something devoid of any kind of experience. It would seem bizarre to attribute subjective experience to large-scale physical objects. As Whitehead once remarked 'Take these chairs – they look pretty stupid.' But these are *societies* of actual entities, and the claim is that with the basic actual entities the situation may be different.

However, he repudiated the term 'pan-psychism', possibly because this suggested a stronger view of minds than he wanted. His view of mind and body was a unified one in which 'mind' stands for mental functioning. It certainly does not stand for a distinct mental substance. Indeed, he rejected the notion of 'substance' as a distinct something which is a bearer of properties and attributes, and also attacked the philosophical adequacy of the Subject-Predicate form of proposition which he held suggested this. Instead he advocated a logic of propositional functions, taking the general form φx, where φ signifies some form of action or occurrence and x signifies that there is someone or something which satisfies this. So φx, where φ means walking, becomes 'There is someone who is walking'. This kind of Logic may indeed be more adequate to the metaphysical shape of a Whiteheadian world of events than that of subjects and predicates. The difficulty is that in writing about it, at any rate in English, it is very difficult to avoid using a Subject-Predicate form of sentence, and nor in fact does Whitehead do so.

In an excellent article 'The Subjectivist Principle and the Linguistic Turn',[6] written before he went deconstructivist, Richard Rorty takes Whitehead up on his claim that the Subject-Predicate form of language is inadequate where statements are made from within the experience of a subject (in the sense of a unique experiencer) with a uniquely occurring experience of an object. But if I see this shape as round (my example) you may also see it as round (or you may not). The proposition 'This shape is round' can mean the same to each of us and be true or false. So the Subject-Predicate form of ordinary language need not distort the truth and what Whitehead wants to bring out in his Subjectivist Principle can be provided for under the notion of token reflexivity. Token reflexive statements are those whose truth conditions have reference to a particular speaker or to a particular place or time, and so include indexicals such as 'I', 'here', 'now'. So 'I am now seeing this shape as round' can be true even if 'This shape is not round' is also true. Rorty thinks that to recognize the importance of token-reflexivity can allow us to retain the Subject-Predicate form of statements of ordinary language. I think this is right, but I do not think that what Whitehead was contending for in his Subjectivist principle can be dealt with simply by taking the linguistic turn. He was after something inescapably metaphysical: the ascription of an inner aspect in all actualities. Whitehead, in fact, rather than speaking of the Subject-Object form of experience, often spoke of the Subject-Superject. According to this doctrine of immanence a subject was incorporated into others and they into it. I find great difficulty in this, but he laid stress on it – he said, it is how in talking to ourselves we talk to the world.

He speaks of this subjective experience as 'feeling' and the datum which is experienced is also a 'feeling'. There are, I think, grave difficulties over this metaphysical view, but it is there. Whitehead himself said that, whereas Kant had written a Critique of Pure Reason, his aim was to write a Critique of Pure Feeling. 'Feeling' is indeed a technical term for some datum being incorporated into the ongoing experience of a subject,[7] and it is used both of the experience of the subject and of what is experienced. But I think it carries with it a number of misleading associations. If a technical term is needed to describe an experiencing subject forming itself out of its experienced relationships with others, I prefer Whitehead's expression 'a concrescence of prehensions'. This may sound like jargon, or it can be a good term for a novel concept. Some of Whitehead's special terms may seem jargon-like, but it is often

possible to see an appropriate meaning by looking at their Latin or
Greek roots. So a 'concrescence' is a growing together and a
'prehension' is a grasping of something which is then appropriated.
An ordinary language word like 'feelings', used in a special sense
cannot be unpacked like this, and can be misleading. However,
sometimes Whitehead uses ordinary language terms in a special
technical sense which can be got at by looking at the root derivation.
So when actual entities develop towards their 'satisfaction', this does
not mean a state in which they will feel content, but one in which
they will be made complete (from *satis* and *factum*). But this use of
ordinary words in non-ordinary senses can make for difficulties,
especially if the switch cannot be detected by looking at the root of
the word. This, I think, is notoriously so in the case of the word
'feeling'.

The immanence of 'feelings' of an actual entity in its successors is
said to secure the identity of 'enduring objects' seen as routes of
actual entities. In my book I had suggested that this identity in a
route of actual entities over time might be thought of as the repetition
of a form. But this was repudiated by Whitehead in the letter I quoted
earlier. If Whitehead had only meant that there was a transfer of
character, and if he had been writing in a later generation, he might
have drawn on the Communications Theory language of information, where structure as well as energy is transmitted. But it is
evident from his letter that this would not have satisfied him. He
wants to maintain a presence of one thing in another, and is trying
to do this through the psycho-physiological term 'feeling', and
perhaps drawing on its twofold meaning, as an act of feeling and as
something which is felt.

These and other difficulties come to a head in Whitehead's Natural
Theology. Whitehead saw Natural Theology as metaphysics and any
concept of God which such a theology may contain should be
required by a metaphysical theory and exemplify its principles.
Whitehead's own metaphysical theory was one of a world which
was a process of becoming of countless actual entities, each a 'concrescence of prehensions', a coming together of a new unity out of
the way in which it unifies its active responses to the rest of its world.
The process, also called 'the passage of nature', is 'an advance into
novelty', where 'novelty' does not merely have the trivial sense of
something happening which had not happened before, but of a new
happening as having its own original character. Whitehead called
what he held to be the basic requirement for this kind of process 'the

category of the ultimate'.[8] This combines the notions of 'creativity', 'one' and 'many', with a process in which each occurrent is a unification of its *many* relata into a *one* with its own novelty. (Whitehead once said to me that his metaphysics was 'a defence of liberalism'.) But also, as I have said, he always insisted that for a world to be possible there must be a basic uniform structure. This is not provided by creativity alone. He speaks of creativity as protean: it allows for the possibility of something to happen but not of anything in particular. Yet a world has to be a particular world and this means that besides creativity it needs some basic structure. Whitehead calls this 'the Primordial Nature of God'. This is not an actuality, still less a 'person'. It is perhaps possible to think of the Primordial Nature of God as a kind of propositional function, a cosmic φx, where φ is the pattern of a predicate and x stands for all the actualities in the world which are values satisfying it. But Whitehead also gives his Primordial Nature of God an 'appetition' to become actual. This, I should have thought, can only be done by combining it with Creativity. He calls it 'an aim at value'. This plays on an ambiguity between 'value' as the ethically neutral notion of a value of the variable x in the propositional function, and 'value' as something which is thought of as good or worth achieving. Be this as it may, the 'appetition' for value in the case of God, as in the case of all other actualities, is satisfied through incorporating its responses to all other actualities in its own developing nature. This developing nature is called 'the Consequent Nature of God'. It prehends all the other actualities which are arising and perishing, and as with all prehensions, incorporates them as data into its own developing nature. This is called 'objectification', and it gives the actualities which are subjectively coming into being and perishing, an 'objective immortality' as taken up into the Consequent Nature of God. I think there are enormous difficulties in this, as there are in Whitehead's general view of how one thing becomes 'objectified' in others. I cannot go into these difficulties in detail here.[9] I find they are largely overlooked by those Process Theologians who fasten onto Whitehead.

I think of Whitehead's God as rather like a cosmic Proust, *à la recherche du temps perdu*, surveying all the scenes and personalities of his past and weaving them into a vast narrative. But Proust's is a *narrative*, not a perpetuation by actual incorporation of the past in the present. I can think of perpetuation of the past not as incorporation into a present actuality, but as a matter of causal influence, memory, tradition, historical narrative. This would of course water down Whitehead's view; the objective immanence of the things which have perished in others which are in process of becoming was a matter of great importance to him. Others may be able, and indeed have been able, to make more of it that I have, notably Professor Hartshorne, who even dismisses Whitehead's notion of 'subjective perishing' in favour of a total preservation of the past in his evolving God. But Whitehead insists that all actual entities perish subjectively while being given objective immortality in the Consequent Nature of God. This incidentally pinpoints a difficulty in how God can be, as Whitehead insists, an actual entity having the same general properties as all actual entities, since He (*sic*) never perishes (and so presumably cannot be prehended by others).

However, I do not want to end on a negative note. I have found much richness in Whitehead's views. Among the features which have remained with me are the basic intuition of Nature as *something going on*, and the consequent emphasis on *processes*, in whose course there is a derivation from the past and anticipation of the future. We need metaphysical ways of expressing transition and continuity, and these are not I think, adequately provided for by sequences of distinct events. Also, as I have said, I find the notion of a conscrescence of prehensions helpful, at any rate as regards the development of biological and personal forms of life. Whether it is applicable at every level of Nature is another matter.

After a long interval I tried to give my own views on these matters in *The Passage of Nature* (1992). (The title is borrowed from an expression of Whitehead's.) I called the book 'a non-Whiteheadian treatment of some Whiteheadian themes'. In this chapter I have touched briefly, with many omissions, on some of these as he expressed them himself. Of course, I have simplified and may well have distorted them. I therefore end with quoting what he said should be the motto of every natural philosopher: 'Seek simplicity and distrust it.'

6

Politics and Philosophy in the 1930s: John Macmurray and Reinhold Niebuhr

I came back from America in 1930, and after a year as a stand-in at Somerville College and another spell in the Rhondda Valley, I was appointed lecturer in philosophy at the Armstrong College, Newcastle-upon-Tyne (now the University of Newcastle, but then a part of the University of Durham). One of the other applicants was Con Drury, and in his 'Conversations with Wittgenstein' he records that 'on several occasions in later years he used to say to me that I owed a great debt to Miss Emmett [*sic*], in that she had saved me from becoming a professional philosopher'.[1] For better or worse, I was now set on that path. There is a genuine problem over philosophy becoming a profession. Over my lifetime I have seen standards of criticism get higher and higher and distinctions of meanings more and more strict, and this is surely right and proper. But this has gone along with a narrowing of the range of subjects discussed, so that philosophy becomes more an in-group pursuit of philosophers than part of general intellectual life. One sign of this is that philosophy books, other than those whose authors are household names, are now seldom reviewed in the national press or in periodicals other than the philosophy journals. I do not know the answer to this. We cannot relax the effort after greater precision, but we could perhaps be more alert to wider problems of public concern. Some, of course, are aware of this; Mary Warnock, for instance, while no longer pursuing philosophy professionally, brings a trained philosopher's mind to bear on difficult questions of public ethics, and Mary Midgly scents out uncritical intrusions of 'scientism' into areas of contemporary thought.

In the 1930s, however, philosophy was less precise and less ingrown and most philosophers were less specialized. In the civic universities a philosophy department establishment normally consisted of a professor and a lecturer – one man and his dog. In Newcastle I was the dog, the man being Louis Arnaud Reid, a moralist and aesthetician. There were fewer students than there have been since the war, but between us we had to cover the subject. I did several courses in political philosophy, always one of my interests, and in the 1930s this was not only an interest but a preoccupation.

I look back on the 1930s as the unhappiest time of my life – not in my personal circumstances, because I was thoroughly enjoying myself in Newcastle, but in respect of what was going on in the world, and the chilling uncertainty as to what ought or could be done about it. It was the time of the rise and increasing encroachment of Hitler's Nazi Germany, of the arrival of Jewish refugees, of increasing widespread unemployment at home. And over everything, there loomed the threat of war, and the belief that if it came we would all be likely to be bombed to destruction in a very short time. This country was singularly unprepared; there were strong pacifist pressures and no clear policy on rearmament.

A number of intellectuals were turning to Marxism, thinking that this was the one force which could withstand Fascism and also contained a coherent political creed. There were self-confessed Communists, but also a number of liberal intellectuals were fellow-travellers. (I believe that this is how the term 'fellow-travellers' came into currency.) Prominent writers, such as Bernard Shaw and Sidney and Beatrice Webb looked to the Soviet Union as the vanguard of civilization. I had been sufficiently inured by my experience of living among Communists in South Wales, and still more by what I had learned about liberal democracy from Lindsay, not to be tempted to fall for Marxism. But a fair amount of time in my political philosophy classes was taken up by arguments with Marxist or would-be Marxist students who opted for economic determinism and the class war.

Among those who faced this issue publicly and head-on were John Macmurray and Reinhold Niebuhr, both of whom I knew. So I shall say something in detail about each of them.

John Macmurray was a philosophy don at Balliol when I was up in the 1920s. He was a highly charismatic figure. In his appearance and also in the burden of his teaching he had a close resemblance to D.H. Lawrence, and I think he cultivated this. In his moral philosophy he was urging us to look honestly at our emotions, and to find freedom in following them, rather than in trying to observe the 'slave morality' of duty which was dictated by abstract reason. This was a strong counter-blast to the kind of moral philosophy we got from Prichard and Ross. The lectures by Macmurray which I attended were not on ethics but on Kant's *Critique of Pure Reason*, and we were given a rather heady version of Kant. Later I came to realize that John Macmurray's interpretations of philosophers tended to be constructions based on a few things they had said. In an essay for Lindsay, I produced a view allegedly from the *Critique of Pure Reason*. Lindsay said 'Where did you get hold of that idea?' and when I said 'From Mr Macmurray's lecture' he laughed, as though that explained it. I found that it was said in Balliol that John had not read further than the Preface to the Second Edition of the *Critique of Pure Reason*, and on the basis of this he constructed a great view of what Kant really meant. This may be an unfair suspicion, but it is not unfair to think that a number of John's views were sweeping and only took account of part of the data.

In the 1930s he became Professor of Philosophy at University College, London, and gave widely attended lectures in which he expounded the difference between what he saw as the 'organic' Marxist view of society and his own view of a community of persons. He gave a number of talks on his personalist ethics, which were published in the book *Freedom and the Modern World* (Faber and Faber, London, 1932). He tilted at our insincerity and fear in acknowledging and expressing our emotions, especially in our suppressing the fear of death, which he himself had faced many times in the trenches, where he had had a very tough war. We are afraid of emotion, he said and we split our intellect and our feelings. The aim was to achieve a loving relationship with other people, and this was a matter of going out to them in a spirit of appreciative awareness. Freedom is described as a spontaneous response to the objective reality of another person.

Macmurray's views on a community of persons in relation to other persons came out in the 1930s in a number of short and somewhat impressionistic books, and had often been given as talks on the BBC. They were worked out in a more sustained way in his Gifford Lectures, *The Self as Agent* (Faber and Faber, London, 1957) and *Persons in Relation* (Faber and Faber, London, 1961). These were given 20 years later when he was Professor of Moral Philosophy in Edinburgh, but in the remarks, whether critical or appreciative, I shall make about the kind of things he was saying in the 1930s it is only right and proper to draw on this fuller treatment.

I was once in Professor Ryle's room, and as Editor of *Mind*, he had a shelf of books which had been sent for review. Pointing to Macmurray's *The Self as Agent*, Ryle said 'When I give my Gifford Lectures I shall take that title, but separate the syllables in the last word.' I have told this to present-day followers of Macmurray, and the phrase 'the self as a gent' has now got into circulation. I doubt whether Macmurray would have accepted it as an appropriate soubriquet; a gent would be likely to be more reticent about expressing his emotions, and, while he would show consideration for people, he might well have a sense of duty.

Macmurray's own title was designed to challenge the traditional standpoint in philosophy, which he held had been a theoretical one. We should start from 'the primacy of the practical'. One might want to say 'Haven't we been here before?', in the various forms of pragmatism, not to mention Marxism. The main difference, I think, is that these look on theory as subordinate to practice and on truth as meaningful when effective in practice. Macmurray fastened on actions as not only guided by reflection but as only possible because carried out by *agents*. 'The primacy of the practical' becomes the primacy of agents acting (as they only can act) in co-operation with other agents. So his real concern was with 'Persons in Relation' (the title of his second volume). He distinguishes mechanical, organic and personal forms of relationship. In the 'mechanical' mode another person is looked on as an object, subject to laws of cause and effect. In the organic mode one person's purposes are furthered through association with another person, or the purposes of both may be furthered, as in exchanges or under contracts or in co-operation for a common end. The personal mode is where one person is related to another without any end or purpose beyond mutual recognition and appreciation. Macmurray however was not a pure 'I-thou' philosopher. He was aware of the necessity for organic functional relations, and of the need for a political order to give stability and bring some measure of justice into them. But this is subsidiary to developing a community of persons in full relation to each other. Macmurray believed this begins in infants; they do not start as little animals who gradually acquire personality. From the beginning their dependence on other people and the growth of mutual communication is more than a merely organic biological relationship. He was aware of the mixture of love, hate and fantasy which may have roots in these early relationships. What he had to say about these recalls the teachings of Melanie Klein rather than of Freud, and what he had to say about adult relationships fits with the views of Personalist Psychologists.

I think, however, that in looking on full personal relations, when they can be achieved, as ends in themselves, and distinguishing them from 'mechanical' or 'organic' relationships, Macmurray failed to do justice to a rightly impersonal aspect in such relationships. Does not an enduring personal relationship need outward-looking interests which are not just personal – public affairs, ideas, music for instance – which we can enjoy in common? These things must be allowed to have, as von Hügel put it, 'each their own inside' which must be respected, and this is not done by treating them as means to personal relations. It might be unfair to suggest that Macmurray was looking for a kind of perpetual honeymoon in human relations. But I think he did not sufficiently allow for a positive value of impersonal interests in enriching such relations, and perhaps also as necessary for their health.

His distinction between personal relations and functional ones shows no awareness of the subtleties of role relations. He uses the word 'hypocritical' in its play-acting sense. But role activity can be personal and sensitive as well as carrying its own morality, which consists in recognizing the particular obligations and restraints appropriate to particular kinds of relationship – that of doctor to patient for instance, or teacher to pupil. Macmurray considers a hypothetical case where a teacher notices abnormal behaviour in a pupil and he says that the teacher will have to switch temporally from a 'personal' relation to the pupil to a 'mechanical' one in which he looks on the pupil as an 'object' whose abnormalities he tries to understand with the help of such psychological knowledge as he has. But this dichotomy surely will not do. A teacher occupies a role in which his relation to his pupils is not a purely personal one. In class he has to maintain a certain amount of what Talcott Parsons called 'affective neutrality', however much he may like some of them better than others. Moreover, he must be trying to get them to learn the subject. Even in the case where he has to bring psychiatrical knowledge to bear on abnormal behaviour this does not mean he is then treating the pupil as an object, laying aside a relation to him as a person. There are, of course, problems here in professional ethics of which doctors as well as teachers are aware. A doctor can have an attitude of what Robert Merton, writing about professions, has called 'detached sensitivity', and this is not just a bedside manner.

So I do not think that Macmurray saw far enough into the impersonal in the personal or the personal in the impersonal. He speaks of the 'inclusion of the negative in the positive', but this somewhat Hegelian expression is used with insufficient explanation to be helpful. There is no treatment, for instance, of the place of discretion in role activity. I did some thinking about this on my own part later on when I was in Manchester having a good deal to do with functional sociologists as well as trying to come to terms with Michael Polanyi's view of personal knowledge, and I shall write about both of these concerns in a later context.

My engagement with Macmurray was mainly in the 1920s and 1930s, but I used to see him from time to time throughout his life, both when he was in Edinburgh and when he was living in retirement in Jordans. Although what he was saying philosophically left a good deal more to be said, I do not want to end on a negative note. I find there is a revival of interest in him at present and his books are being republished. Tony Blair is reported to have said that Macmurray is the philosopher of his choice. And Dame Cicely Saunders, the founder of the Hospice Movement for the care of the terminally ill, said in a lecture which I attended that it was Macmurray's books which gave her the moral backing she needed for her own work and that she tried to introduce her colleagues to them. Neither of these is likely to underestimate the importance of impersonal matters, whether Tony Blair in struggling with public affairs or Cicely Saunders in drawing on medical expertise. Both of these are dedicated to working for a community of persons in differing and difficult settings. If they find philosophical support in Macmurray's books for making 'community' and 'persons' more than just buzz words, that is fine. Critical comments can be left to others with more leisure.

However, the question which preoccupied many of us in the 1930s was not that of persons in community but of what to do in a world which seemed to be heading for disaster. Some liberal intellectuals, as I have said, looked to Marxism as the main force to counter this, while others tried to meet the situation with a peace-loving personal morality strongly laced with feelings of guilt. Germany, they thought, had been wronged in the settlement of the 1914–18 war, and if we were now nice to Hitler, he would be nice to us. The Peace Pledge Union, calling on people to renounce war unconditionally, was running strong. Stanley Baldwin, speaking of the General

Election of 1935 when he was returned as Prime Minister, said that
the electorate would not have stood for proposals for rearmament.

For me, the person who chiefly spoke to our condition in the 1930s
was Reinhold Niebuhr. He was an American of German Lutheran
background, and he operated from a chair in Christian Ethics in the
Union Theological Seminary, New York. Thus he could be
considered a theologian rather than a philosopher, but he once
described himself as 'a moralist who had strayed into theology', and
he struggled with problems about the nature of corporate morality
which philosophers need to take note of and which not very many
of them do. He came to be seen (though unjustly) in some quarters
not so much as a teacher of public morality as public amorality. This
may have been suggested by the title of his widely influential book,
Moral Man and Immoral Society. It came out in 1932, the same year as
Macmurray's *Freedom and the Modern World*. They could hardly have
been more different. Niebuhr was attacking the simplistic liberal
morality which failed to realize the intransigence of group relations
and the impossibility of simply meeting this intransigence with
principles of personal morality. Among his principal targets were the
moralistic utterances on international affairs produced by successive
American Administrations. He attacked the notion that idealism in
morality, along with advances in the social sciences, could meet the
problems produced by clashes of interests in power politics. And
politics necessarily involves getting and using power in the
protection and promotion of interests, including what is perceived
as the public interest. This does not mean that there is no morality,
but what is moral must be part of 'the art of the possible' within the
constraints and pressures of corporate actions. There are several
implications of this. One is that those responsible for group activities
cannot be altruistic in the way in which individuals can: they cannot,
for instance, be generous with other people's money. If the members
of the group as a whole back generous action, that is different. But
this is not often likely. Another is that those in positions of public
responsibility are expected to safeguard or promote the corporate
interests, even where the groups concerned may not have been deliberately set up for this purpose. (So however much successive Foreign
Secretaries may proclaim loyalty to the European Union, they couple
this with saying that their first concern will be to safeguard British
interests.) Another factor is that the interests of different groups in
their relations with other groups are seldom harmonious, hence
competition and clashes of power. Niebuhr thought that American

Liberals were not sufficiently prepared to accept this, and looked to a Utopian harmony, particularly if people accepted the American democratic way of life. Europeans have probably never been as starry-eyed, and have been more pragmatic in their approach to politics.

The two enemies of political morality are moralism and cynicism, and in seeing the inadequacies of the former it is all too easy to swing to the latter. Niebuhr's principal target was moralism which I understand as a simple belief in the applicability of personal moral principles in public matters. He was therefore often accused of cynicism. But he was not cynical or Machiavellian (in the popular sense of the word, which may not be altogether right for Machiavelli himself). He saw that politics was concerned with getting and using power in the protection and furthering of interests, but there may also be a claim to promote the public interest. This need not be hypocritical, though 'the public interest' will be likely to be seen from a point of view which is not completely objective and disinterested. (This was Rousseau's problem over the General Will.) Niebuhr saw this as an argument for democracy, a pluralistic democracy in which different groups with their partial points of view encountered each other within a framework of law. As Madison observed in *The Federalist*, 'factions' need not be disruptive provided that there are enough of them; their conflicts of interests make them unlikely to gang up together against the unorganized.

Niebuhr has a powerful defence of democracy in a small book *The Children of Light and the Children of Darkness* (London and N.Y., 1945). The morality of the Children of Light is based on a belief in the goodness of human nature; the Children of Darkness base their conduct on self-interest. The title comes from St Luke's Gospel 16.8 where Christ wryly observes that 'the children of this world' (Niebuhr's 'children of darkness') 'are in their generation wiser than the children of light'. This is because the children of this world can be more realistic that the children of light, who can be sentimental. But 'realism' in situations can be ruthlessness as well as objective appraisal. Niebuhr was continually insisting that we realize that every moral attitude has its own forms of conception. Democracy is not a pure means to a harmonious way of life. It is 'a method of finding proximate solutions to insoluable problems' (op. cit., p. 83), 'insoluble' because in public and political life the attempt to solve one problem such as securing full employment, is likely to produce another, perhaps inflation. This is my example, not Niebuhr's; I do not think that selecting a presently topical example affects his view, since he was saying that life is like this, and I think he was right.

Democracy is not therefore a way of securing a harmonious society in which all can realize their potentials. People have a potential capacity to want the good of others beside themselves, and they also have a potential one for self-aggrandisement, and the latter infects the former as well as the former putting constraints on the latter. Democracy is a system which draws on such resources as there may be in promoting the former and curbing the latter. Hence 'man's capacity for justice makes democracy possible; but man's capacity for injustice makes democracy necessary' (op. cit., p. vi). This is a long way from an idealistic advocacy of democracy, but it is nonetheless a strong one. There is also the need for toleration, not only because the maintenance of a peaceful society demands that we believe that other people's views should not be forcibly suppressed, but because we know that we ourselves, as well as our opponents, are caught in a web of self-deception over the absolute righteousness of our own causes. When we fail to see this, we can see our opponents as demons, as they also may see us.

Both Niebuhr and Macmurray were tilting at moralism and idealistic Utopianism, and were doing so in the 1930s, when, as I have said, left-wing liberal intellectuals were sympathetic to Marxist socialism. Macmurray had his criticisms of Marxism, but yet held that Communism was a movement within history directed to a universal society of human brotherhood. It differed from Christianity in not being based on love in human relations; nevertheless, he could speak of the USSR as 'the most democratic society there has ever been' – and that in the period of Stalin's trials. Niebuhr was more realistic about the ruthlessness of Russian Communism, and also of the Utopian illusion that this ruthlessness was only a temporary stage of transition to a classless society in which the State would wither away. Classes were not the only groups through which people tried to further their interests. Some groups may displace others, but the problems in the use of power in collective activities will remain.

Niebuhr's problems over the adequacy of personal moralism was not only a matter of the difficulty of pursuing the public interest in a sphere in which groups pursue the interests of their members, and often justifiably so. This might be seen as a secular problem in group dynamics. He was also struggling with the ways in which the deceitfulness of the human heart infects personal as well as collective morality. Here he spoke as a religious moralist.

As a religious moralist, and still more as a Christian one, he looks for a transcendent dimension for morality. That we do not achieve the perfect society or even perfect and final solutions to particular moral problems, is not only because of shortcomings in our knowledge, to be remedied perhaps by advances in the social sciences, nor in the combination of this with distorting effects of our own interests and those of our groups, to be corrected perhaps by better analytic self-knowledge. There are limitations due to the very nature of our bounded existence which prevents us from achieving ideal solutions which will be lasting solutions. Niebuhr speaks of our decisions and actions as infected by sin; it is not always clear how he distinguishes distortions due to sin and those due simply to the fact of finiteness which is not our fault. He would have met this, I think, by saying the main root of sin is *pride*, in our unwillingness to acknowledge our limitations, so that we overrate the rightness of our decisions and our principles in seeking power to impose them on others. Yet he also believed that a good deal of vitality in personal life goes with this assertiveness. There is no easy solution. A transcendent dimension of morality can introduce reference to a perfection which we cannot realize in our limited conditions, but which we can look to in passing judgement on anything which we achieve. I myself have tried to interpret this transcendent reference philosophically in terms of Kant's conception of the Regulative Ideal, which cannot in principle be fully instantiated, but which gives an orientation to our practical reason.[2] In writing about this in a very different vein from Niebuhr, and in using it to criticize Utopian views of society, I have been conscious of what I learned from him about the right and the wrong use of moral absolutes. There is a good deal of Utopianism about. When I taught political theory I used to say to students that in politics there was a catch in everything – which does not mean there are not better and worse decisions.

For Niebuhr the absolute reference was to the Love of God, and he saw a pointer to this in the extreme demands of some of the moral teaching of the Gospels. I referred to this quality in Christian ethics in connection with Lindsay's view of 'the Two Moralities'.[3] For Lindsay there was the morality of grace, shown in personal acts of generosity, and the morality of reciprocal give and take, which could be a practicable standard in a common life. Lindsay saw the ethics of the Sermon on the Mount and the command 'Be ye perfect' as belonging to the personal morality of grace. He speaks of gracious acts, not done only by saints but by ordinary people, going beyond the morality of the world of claims and counterclaims. Niebuhr saw even the morality of saints as carrying its own imperfections, and looked for grace through humility and penitence. His morality of grace will not therefore be a distinct form of personal action; it will be a matter of looking beyond anything which we can possibly achieve. He respected idealists such as pacifists, as witnesses to the transcendent element in morality, but those realistically engaged in the art of the possible would have to be prepared to get their hands dirty.

In *An Interpretation of Christian Ethics* (New York: Harpers, 1935 after *Moral Man and Immoral Society*) he takes Christian Ethics as pointing to what he calls (perhaps rather rhetorically) 'the impossible possibility'. 'Impossible' can indicate that the ideal is transcendent and so never fully to be realized. 'Possibility' can indicate that we can set it in our sights while seeking proximate solutions to the problems of our world. In this we should not take just any means, regardless of moral considerations but we should take practicable means, and this may sometimes mean a choice of evils including the used of force. The problems are unlikely to stay solved, and the solutions may bring other problems in their wake. But to keep the transcendent reference can save us from thinking that the success of our actions is the be-all-and-end-all of our efforts and save us from swinging between pride in what we can achieve and despair about what we cannot.

Niebuhr summed this up in what I find a memorable passage:[4]

Humanity always faces a double task. The one is to reduce the anarchy of the world to some kind of immediately sufferable order and unity; and the other is to set these tentative and insecure unities and achievements under the criticism of the ultimate ideal. When they are not thus challenged, what is good in them becomes evil and each tentative harmony becomes the cause of a new anarchy. With Augustine we must realize that the peace of the world is gained by strife. That does not justify us either in rejecting such a tentative peace or in accepting it as final. The peace of the city of God can use and transmute the lesser and insecure peace of the city of the world; but that can be done only if the peace of the world is not confused with the ultimate peace of God.

I listened to an address by Niebuhr in July 1939. He had just come back from a visit to Germany, and, bilingual as he was, he had been talking to a number of people and sizing up the situation. He painted a terrifying picture, and was convinced that war would break out, as indeed it did two months later. The text of his address was 'We are perplexed, but not in despair'. Behind the horror and the anxiety there was still the 'impossible possibility' of the ultimate peace of God. I took the memory of that address with me into the War.

I got to know Reinhold Niebuhr better and more personally after the War, and I stayed with him and his wife in New York. His English wife, Ursula, was a theologian in her own right and had been my near contemporary at Oxford. We still keep in touch by correspondence. Reinhold had had a stroke which severely curtailed his activities. For some time this led to frustration and exasperation. Then I found that a jollier and more relaxed Reinhold had come out. I remarked on this to his brother, Richard Niebuhr, who said yes, but only after he had come to accept that he could no longer be the world-star preacher and prophet. Instead, people came and talked to him at home, and his advice was regularly sought by members of the Kennedy Administration. He was a good man, and I think he had a touch of greatness.

7

Samuel Alexander
in Manchester

I went to the University of Manchester in the autumn term 1938. I already knew Manchester, as my sister and brother-in-law lived there; they were neighbours of Samuel Alexander, and when visiting them I used to see him and we struck up a friendship. On my appointment he wrote me a charming letter:

> How I rejoice! For the University because it gets you ... For you because you will be much freer now to work out your future in the way you like best; and I believe in your future. And selfishly for myself because I shall have the chance of seeing you and cheering my old days with being your colleague, and ever your affectionate
>
> S. Alexander.

It was not to be. Alexander died during the summer vacation before I got to Manchester. But I can write from my recollections and also from those of other people in Manchester, where he was a beloved, indeed almost a legendary, figure.

Alexander was born in Australia in 1859 and educated at Wesley College, Melbourne. He then came to Oxford in 1877 and sat for a scholarship at Balliol. He found himself sitting next to George Curzon (later to be 'George Nathaniel Curzon, a most superior person' of the Masque of Balliol, and finally Foreign Secretary and Viceroy of India). He remarked 'I don't think Mr Alexander is going to get a scholarship.' Alexander did, and Curzon did not. When Alexander took pupils in philosophy, Curzon was the first. Subsequently he must have asked Curzon to write in support of his application for the Chair in Manchester, since a letter from Curzon (12 February 1888) regrets that he had been unable to do so because he had been abroad, but adds that he considered that 'anything related to Philosophy and signed by me would not have improved your chances. Do you remember how backward I was?' The rude schoolboy had learnt whom to respect.

Alexander took Firsts in Classical Moderations and Greats and also in Mathematical Moderations. The latter was a sign of his interest in natural science, and this was further shown when, having won a Fellowship in Lincoln College (the first Jew to be awarded a Fellowship at an Oxford or Cambridge college), he resigned in order to study psychology. He spend the winter of 1890–91 in Münsterberg's laboratory in Freiburg-im-Bresgau acquainting himself with experimental work.

In 1893 he was appointed to the Chair of Philosophy in the University of Manchester. One of the other candidates was G.F. Stout (later Professor at Saint Andrew's). Alexander has an account of what happened when they were waiting to be interviewed.

> Now Mr Stout, in the days before he came under the control of Mrs Stout, was negligent of his appearance, and he came to the final interview with the Council with his neck-tie riding half-way up his collar. I told him he would never be taken in that condition and set his neck-tie right; but apparently thinking it unfair to take advantage of the offices of a rival, he deliberately tore it back to its old place, and this act cost him the election. The Council rightly decided that its professor of philosophy should set an example in a well-dressed university.[1]

Mrs Stout, when told this story, is said to have commented 'The impudence of *him* talking about well-dressed men.' There is a story, however, which shows that Alexander had his own sense of what was proper in the way of dress. He used to transport himself everywhere on what became a celebrated bicycle. On one occasion he bicycled to Liverpool for a philosophy meeting. There was a dinner after the meeting, and Alexander was asked about his dress suit (those were the formal days). He pointed to his cycling tweeds and said 'Underneath'. It was necessary to stay the night and Alexander, on being asked if he had any pyjamas, pointed to his suit and said 'Underneath' again.

Alexander lived in Manchester for the rest of his life, including retirement, until his death in 1938. He never married, and shared a house with his brother. He has been called one of the great solitaries in philosophy. This might be said of his philosophy, which was a unique system, not to be classified as belonging to any school. It can also be said of his way of life; he was single-mindedly dedicated to philosophy. This was not that his philosophy was narrow – far from it – but he developed it in his own room in Manchester. He did not, I think, travel much, or go about to conferences and meet other philosophers. He did, however, write letters as also did they. The University Library in Manchester has an archive of extensive correspondence with letters from many of the main figures in British Philosophy at the time: F.H. Bradley, Bernard Bosanquet, Bertrand Russell, G.F. Stout, H.H. Joachim, H. Wildon Carr, F.C.S. Schiller, H.W.B. Joseph, R.G. Collingwood, James Ward, and, of an older generation, Herbert Spencer and Leslie Stephen. Among scientists, there are letters from C. Lloyd-Morgan and Charles Sherrington. We are unlikely to see another such archive. The letters discuss each other's work and are nearly all written by hand. Nowadays people are more likely to ring up, or go about and meet each other. Also, those in University jobs have little leisure for carrying on this kind of intellectual correspondence.

There is a splendid bust of Alexander by Epstein in the entrance hall of the Arts Building of the University of Manchester. Replying at its presentation, Alexander spoke gratefully of the affection he was shown by his colleagues, pupils and friends.

> I cannot tell how I have won this affection; unless it be that I possess a fair stock of affection myself, which extends to all children and to dogs and cats and other animals. Apart from that, after careful self-examination, I can only conclude that there must be something in me which in the eighteenth century they used to call *je ne sais quoi*. … Though I shall be glad if it is said of me, 'He was known for a certain gaiety of speech,' I prefer to have it said of me, 'He contrived for some years to persuade people that he could think.' For, my Lord, in spite of appearances to the contrary, I am really and truly and fundamentally a very serious man; it is only that I find it difficult to be dull. How accurately the artist has entered into my character is shown by his giving the portrait just a touch of mulish obstinacy, which is perhaps less known to my friends than it is to myself in the secret places of my heart.

He added that

In the future when I am forgotten this bust will be described among the University's possessions as the bust of a professor, not otherwise now remembered, except as an ingredient of the ferment which the earlier years of the twentieth century cast into speculation, but it will be added that it is an Epstein.[2]

When the Joint Session of the Mind Association and the Aristotelian Society was held in Manchester in 1946, I took a number of the members to see the bust. As they were standing round the hall of the Arts Building someone remarked 'Never in the history of philosophy did so many Logical Positivists pay tribute to such a metaphysician.' In 1946 'Logical Positivist' was still a title used of the new empiricists, although the strong opposition between them and philosophers whose roots were in older forms was already breaking down. The logical positivist rejection of metaphysics was based on the belief that metaphysics claimed to have knowledge which was *a priori* not only in an analytic sense, but one which claimed to make substantive assertions. Unlike scientific assertions they were not open to verification.

Alexander would have repudiated this sharp distinction. He claimed that, in a wide sense, his metaphysical philosophy was empirical. His use of the term empirical was considerably wider than that of most later empiricists.

> The word empirical must not be too closely pressed. It is intended to mean nothing more than the method used in the special sciences. It is a description of method and not of the subject-matter, and is equivalent to experiential ... Philosophy differs from the sciences nowhere in its spirit but only in its boundaries, in dealing with certain comprehensive features of experience which lie outside the purview of the special sciences.[3]

The special sciences study variable features in a variable world. Philosophy studies pervasive characters of the world, which, as pervasive, Alexander calls *a priori* or categorical. 'These *a priori* elements of the world are, however, experienced just as much as the empirical ones' (that is particular and variable forms of experience). 'Philosophy may therefore be described as the experiential or empirical study of the non-empirical or *a priori*, and of such questions as arise out of the relation of the empirical to the *a priori*. It is thus itself one of the sciences delimited from the others by its special subject-matter.'

I have quoted these sentences from the Introduction to *Space, Time and Deity* to show how he was to connect his metaphysical philosophy with science, seeking to claim that his method of reflection on general characters of experience could be called empirical. There are of course two questions (among others) which can be asked: whether experience in fact has all-pervasive characters and whether the theory of knowledge in which Alexander describes how they are discerned is an acceptable one. In looking at these questions in the context of his philosophy I shall not try to give a summary of a very complex system, any more than I did in the case of Whitehead. I shall simply touch on some of its main features sufficiently to indicate where I think they have a lasting interest and where I find most difficulty in them.

In calling the all-pervasive characters categories, Alexander looks to Kant. For Kant the Categories are *a priori* concepts which the mind uses in interpreting experience as an objective order, while for Alexander they are taken realistically as actual pervasive characters. The list is Kantian: Substance, Cause and Relation; and (here is his greatest innovation) they are characters of Space-Time, which is the basic nature of the world. (For Kant, Space and Time belong to the Transcendental Aesthetic as necessary forms of sensory intuition.) Alexander absolutizes Space-Time and even speaks of it as the fundamental 'stuff' of things. It is a continuum, but a continuum of 'motions', the motions forming complexes (substances) with regularities in the ways in which one motion passes to another (causation).

Alexander claimed support for the concept of the Space-Time continuum in a memoir of 1908 by Minkowski, and he also refers to memoirs by Einstein and Lorentz.[4] These, he said, formed a basis for the theory of General Relativity. His references to General Relativity are respectful but diffident, and he did not come very close to it. In particular he took the differentiation of Space-Time as due not to gravitational forces, but to 'motions', a primitive concept for what he also calls, somewhat poetically, the 'restlessness' of Space-Time. He would not have accepted the view that motion could be defined by alteration of spacio-temporal co-efficients; what Russell called the 'at-at' view where motion consists in a body being at a certain place at a certain time and at another place at another time. Rather, Space-Time itself was in motion, the movement being produced by Time.

Alexander did not, as far as I know, struggle with McTaggart's objections to the notion of an absolute flow of time. He might have replied by saying that Time was not an absolute flow on its own. It was the aspect of the totality of Space-Time which made it a process of transition from one grouping of ordered complexes to another. He said that in this respect Time could be taken as the inner aspect of the totality of Space-Time on analogy with how Mind could be taken as an inner aspect of the totality of our Body-Mind. So 'Time is the Mind of Space' – a semi-serious remark which used to be quoted out of context in the 1930s and held up for special ridicule as a metaphysical remark. There are, of course, enormous problems here, not least over holding that the things which exist in nature are complexes of motions in Space-Time. It would be interesting to have a careful comparison of his view with a General Relativity view of matter as resulting from warping in the geometry of Space-Time (if indeed the analogy is close enough to pursue).

Be this as it may, there is a feature of Alexander's view with which I am very much in sympathy. Whatever the basic nature of the world, a process is going on which gives rise to forms of existence with genuinely new qualities and new capacities. He does not, as far as I know, use the term 'emergence', which was coined by Lloyd Morgan. As with the view which was to be called 'emergence', he held that certain ordered complexes could display new qualities, which depend on underlying qualities, but are not simply epiphenominal (or, as it might now be said, 'supervenient') in being reducible to these. They are new in their causal capacities as well as in their descriptions. These qualities could not have been predicted from the constituent elements out of which the new syntheses arose.

Alexander's view is a naturalistic one, but it is not a reductive naturalism, and still less is it a materialism. 'Matter' is a quality of complexes of Space-Time motions ordered in physical laws. Some complexes of matter have chemical properties, and display the secondary qualities such as colour as well as the primary qualities such as weight. Certain chemical complexes are bearers of a new quality, and become living matter; and certain of these become bearers of a further quality, mind. Mind for Alexander does not stand for a distinct mental factor, still less a distinct kind of substance. It is the name of a new quality manifested by certain neural processes, and in one sense it is identical with its neural and physiological base. But in another sense it is a genuinely new emergent, with the unique characteristic of being conscious. Hence Alexander insisted he was not a behaviourist.

Nor is mind the final emergent property. It is the highest that we know, but Alexander holds that we find an aspiration, a reaching-out towards something yet higher. This will be a further quality which has not yet emerged, and he calls it 'Deity'. 'Deity' is not God as a Being distinct from the world. 'God' is a way of indicating Deity as an as yet unrealized quality. It is also a way of indicating what Alexander calls the 'nisus' of Space-Time. This makes Space-Time productive of more than a kaleidoscopic shift of motions. There is a trend towards the production of new forms of organization displaying new qualities. This involves Time, as the aspect of Space-Time which shows it, to use a phrase of Whitehead's, as 'an advance into novelty'. There is novelty not only in the sense that something happens which had not happened before; there are new syntheses displaying new qualities which can be called higher. The 'nisus' making for these can be said to be a teleological feature of Space-Time. I am not sure by what argument Alexander would justify this teleology, beyond appealing, as he does, to our sense of a trend in which we find ourselves caught up. In finding the spearhead of this in an aspiration towards the as-yet unrealized quality of Deity, his non-existent God is more than a projection produced by dissatisfaction with life as it is. There is the lure of an as yet unrealized possibility, and were it to be realised there would be another beyond it again.

Were it to be realized, then a new quality would have emerged. Alexander does not give it a description. It might perhaps be sanctity, and there might perhaps be premonitions of it in the lives of saints. Alexander speaks of a mystical sense of reverence and refers to what Rudolf Otto in *The Idea of the Holy* called the 'numinous'. In religion he said he was an Ottoman. Towards the end of his life Alexander was awarded the Order of Merit. There is a charming letter in the archive from the Jewish scholar Claude Montefiore. 'You do walk humbly indeed with your funny God, and are so beautifully unconscious that you are *really* a great swell.'

It is time to come back to the nature of Alexander's philosophy. He claimed it was an empirical study discerning pervasive characters in experience. It is difficult to think of these as discerned by a phenomenological description of experience. Rather, we have a bold speculative construction making contact at some places with what can be experienced. This, however, might be enough to satisfy

Alexander, since he says somewhere that all our balloons must be captive balloons. It is more difficult to see how it is justified by his own theory of knowledge. Alexander's opposition to the Idealism from which he had started out in Oxford led him to deny that there was anything in knowledge that the mind constructed. Knowledge was a direct relation, which he called 'compresence', of a mind with an object. (In the case of our own knowledge there is also what he called 'enjoyment', an inner awareness that we are knowing.) 'Compresence' is a relation between things as together, and in the case of knowledge these are a conscious mind and an object. In this relation Alexander says we report with 'natural piety' what we discern by reflective inspection.

The term 'natural piety' is drawn from Wordsworth's poem *The Rainbow*.

> The Child is father of the Man;
> And I could wish my days to be
> Bound each to each by natural piety.

He does not primarily use it in Wordsworth's sense of a reverent joy in nature (though perhaps this too). It is the attitude of mind of simply discerning and accepting what it there. There is a sympathetic and critical discussion of this by Collingwood.[5]

Thus considered, Alexander's metaphysics would seem to be a variety of positivistic metaphysics, whose difference from the commoner varieties consists chiefly in being the work of a very rich, very wise and very profound thinker; but also in a kind of very subtle simplicity, or highly sophisticated *naïveté*, to which the results of intricate research and far-reaching inference appear as perfectly obvious facts which leap to the eyes as soon as they are opened. Alexander's was, in fact, a mind of extraordinary power and energy, and his character one of extraordinary simplicity and candour. ... When he described knowledge as the mere 'compresence' of a mind with an object I can suppose that he was giving a truthful account of his own experience. It was as if he had found words in which to say without offending his own modesty 'put me in front of anything I don't understand, and I will promise to understand it in next to no time'.

Collingwood goes on to say that not only is this not true of the groping character of his own problem-solving, but it would mean that the same set of pervasive characters ought to be recognized *semper, ubique, ab omnibus*, and that this has not been the case.

There are great difficulties over 'compresence' when it comes to having a view of error. In errors and illusions, according to Alexander the mind dislocates and rearranges elements in reality with which it is compresent. Lindsay criticized this in the paper 'What does the Mind construct?' to which I referred in Chapter 3. This 'rearrangement' cannot surely mean, says Lindsay, that when a grey piece of paper is seen green against a red ground 'the mind rummages about the universe until it finds a patch of green of the exact same size wanted and then plonks it down on the patch of grey; but if it does not mean that, what does it mean?' What do these metaphors (if they are metaphors) of 'dislocating' and 'transferring' amount to? 'The paradoxical implication of the argument that when we know we do nothing to objects, seems to be that when we make mistakes and are thoroughly stupid we perform feats in the world of reality which would stagger a Mahatma.'[6]

I think that Lindsay was on the right lines. Knowing does not alter the objective reality which we seek to know. But we construct means of interpretation – models, icons, theories, also representative images, indeed verbal statements – and because we construct them we can manipulate them and can make mistakes with them. Knowledge is not action, but it involves action. Neither Alexander's 'compresence' nor his 'enjoyment' allows for this. He can be called a naïve realist, not because his view lacks sophistication, but because it claims direct apprehension. There is a big price to be paid for this when he comes to explain error.

Alexander considered that Whitehead had superseded him. He remarked that he could say, as Dr Johnson said of himself with regard to Burke, that he had 'rung the bell' for him. But it is not the case that what he had tried to say was to be better said by Whitehead. They have very different systems. One perhaps rather surprising difference is that while Alexander started from his scientific interest in neuro-physiology and ended with something like a General Relativity world of a Space-Time continuum, Whitehead started out as an applied mathematician with an interest in Relativity physics and ended with a world of what seem like psycho-physiological processes. This might suggest that Alexander's world was a barer one than Whitehead's, but there is an important sense in which it is a richer one. Whitehead's world is composed of one type of entity with the same fundamental qualities (though differing in degree). Alexander's world is one in which genuinely new qualities appear at different levels. This was remarked on by Collingwood in a letter in the archive.

> There is still one point in which I think (though I am not sure) *P and R* [*Process and Reality*] fails to take up and develop a leading point in *S.T.D.* [*Space, Time and Deity*]. Your world seems to me a world in which evolution and history have a real place. Whitehead's world is indeed all process, but I don't see this process is in the same way productive or creative of new things (e.g. Life, Mind) arising on the old as on a foundation. W. seems rather to deny that these things are really new at all – at least, he seems to say so pretty explicitly in *Nature and Life*. On that question I am impenitently an Alexandrine. I don't believe that nature is really alive, and all that business, I think it is only a dodge to evade the question, how does anything genuinely new come into existence?

Alexander said once that he had 'a low view of the amoeba'. He insisted on there being genuinely new emergent qualities, and on this, like Collingwood, I would count myself an Alexandrine. The use of the term 'emergence' (not, as I said, Alexander's) might be accused of being a way of baptizing a difficulty rather than explaining it. Whether it is helpful or not, the question is whether such qualities *are* genuinely new or whether they are reducible to more basic ones, as supervenient or epiphenomenal.

Alexander's world also contained 'values'; he called these 'tertiary' qualities. They do not emerge as do the secondary qualities in the world apart from minds, but are found in actual combinations of mind and objects. Goodness occurs in satisfying the affection and desires which make for a harmonious social order; this is how Alexander sees morality. It is fair to say that he did not give a great deal of attention to a view of morality. His primary interest in value was in Beauty, and he wrote and spoke extensively about aesthetics. He believed that we have a particular aesthetic feeling which is aroused and satisfied through works of art. Art grows out of the constructive impulse which we share with birds and animals, to shape materials for practical purposes – birds build their nests and beavers their dams. This constructive impulse can be disengaged from practical uses and become contemplative. It will then be aesthetic pleasure in contemplating significant forms. The term 'significant form' was being used by philosophically-minded artists at the time. The meaning of 'significant' is not altogether clear. In Alexander's use it suggests what Kant said was the character of a work of art: that it displayed purposiveness without purpose. It is something constructed, but it is contemplated and enjoyed without concern for a use. In seeing aesthetic satisfaction in a disinterested contemplation of something constructed, Alexander stressed the importance of the actual activity of constructing: the artist has to work with and manipulate a material medium (which can include words and sounds). He was stressing this at a time when the fashionable theory of aesthetics was that of Croce, in which aesthetic experience is enjoyment of a work of art as something purely internal and spiritual, and the need for a material medium has no part in the theory.

In saying that Beauty is discerned by the practical impulse turned contemplative, Alexander does not deny that some beautiful things also have an essential practical use – buildings, for instance. Alexander had a strong interest in architecture, and I remember he once took me round Manchester – yes, Manchester – pointing out buildings to admire. He drew a distinction between beauty seen displayed in a use and when it is seen without any regard to a use, putting this as a distinction between 'prose and poetry in the arts'. He thought that one could sometimes see a building as 'poetry' not 'prose'; an example was the little lodge, which he loved, at the entrance to Ashburne Hall. (Ashburne Hall is a women's Hall of Residence of the University of Manchester, and Alexander was an honorary Ashburnian.)

His main writings on aesthetics appeared in *Beauty and Other Forms of Value* (London, Macmillan, 1933), the last book published by Alexander himself. Other writings, originally occasional essays and addresses, were published posthumously by John Laird, who introduced them with a Memoir, in *Philosophical and Literary Pieces* (London, Macmillan, 1939). The title indicates that they are not all strictly on philosophy. Some, for instance, on Jane Austen, Molière, Dr Johnson, come out of his wide interest in literature. They are written however with a philosophical turn, and always in a courteous reflective style which is a joy to read. One is on 'Pascal the Writer'. Of Pascal the religious philosopher he once said to me 'He is so satisfying – but quite impossible.' These pieces can be read by anyone with wide intellectual interests but without a special concern for philosophy, while philosophers unable to engage sympathetically with the metaphysical system of *Space, Time and Deity*, may yet find a good deal of contemporary interest in some of the subsidiary discussions throughout that great book, on matters, for instance, such as Universals, Causation, the relation of Body and Mind, and our knowledge of other minds.

There is one respect in which all unbeknown, Alexander may have influenced the course of modern philosophy. The young Wittgenstein was researching in aeronautical engineering in the University of Manchester between 1908 and 1912. The thoughts which he was eventually to work out in the *Tractatus Logico-Philosophicus* were beginning to form in his mind, and he sought out Alexander to talk about them. Alexander is said to have advised him to go and see Frege, calling Frege 'the greatest living philosopher'.[7] Wittgenstein visited Frege, and in the Preface to the *Tractatus* he said that it was Frege and Russell to whom 'I owe in large measure the stimulation of my thoughts'.

Con Drury is reported to have said that Wittgenstein admired the title of *Space, Time and Deity*, and said 'That is where the great problems of philosophy lie.'[8] It is unlikely that he would ever have read the book. Its manner of writing and its conception of what might be an 'empirical' philosophy were very far from what Wittgenstein or indeed most philosophers of a later generation would have counted as empirical. Nor would Wittgenstein have been sympathetic to the way in which Alexander tried to connect philosophy with the sciences. Here however, in his intention if not in his method, he may win sympathy with some of our contemporaries.

8

Philosophy in Manchester:
Religion and Metaphysiscs.
Michael Polanyi

During my time in Newcastle I had been fully occupied with my teaching and outside interests, without very much contact with philosophers elsewhere. I continued to work from the base I had laid down in Oxford, and on the whole I looked on the newer methods, dubbed broadly 'logical positivism', as alien. I was, however, to have one unexpected *avant-garde* encounter. There was a branch of the British Institute (now the Royal Institute) of Philosophy in Newcastle, which brought together colleagues in the College and some from outside it who had an interest in philosophy. I had been its secretary. At some date in the War, when I was in Manchester, I was invited to go up to Newcastle and give a paper to the group. I thought this would be a pleasant opportunity to meet old acquaintances. During the War the meetings, which were then quite small, were held in the flat of a research biochemist, Dr Freda Herbert. When I arrived she said to me 'I hope you won't mind if Wittgenstein comes.' I said *'What!'* Wittgenstein, as is well known, had left Cambridge when the War came and gone to work as a porter in a London hospital. His unit was evacuated to the Royal Victoria Infirmary in Newcastle. Dr Herbert had a laboratory in the Infirmary, and an orderly had come in to borrow some apparatus. They got talking, and being knowledgeable about philosophy, she realized that this was Wittgenstein. She said to him 'We have a philosophy group which is having a meeting on Friday evening. Miss Emmet is coming from Manchester to give us a paper. Would you like to come?' And he did.

I gave my paper, and when it came to discussion, he brushed it aside and the talk centred on him. I cannot remember much that was said, except that for some reason quite unconnected with the paper we got onto what nowadays are called 'out of body experiences', where consciousness seems to be detached and floating free. Freda Herbert, who, as a medical biochemist knew about anaesthetics, told us that in the case of some anaesthetics the higher centres come back before the lower ones, so that one can be conscious without any physical sensation. This interested Wittgenstein; he said he remembered coming to after an operation and 'My soul was a black ghost in the corner of the room, and it gradually came nearer and took possession of my body.' I once told this story in the presence of a somewhat severe American analytic philosopher: she was deeply shocked, and said 'Did he really believe that?' She seemed unable to see that the flavour of an experience could be conveyed by an imaginative manner of speaking.

I was fascinated by seeing Wittgenstein in action, and so did not mind that my paper was disregarded, and I expect that the members of the group felt the same. I have been told, however, that when this happened time after time at the meetings of the Moral Sciences Club in Cambridge, it became embarrassing, and not courteous to the speakers. But one could only learn from Wittgenstein on his own terms.

I was in Manchester through the War, and was reserved to go on with my job. Those who were reserved could be required also to put in a certain number of hours of national service every week. So I was fully occupied, as indeed were most philosophers, and there was not much opportunity for contact. Part of my teaching was in the Philosophy of Religion, in which I had always had an interest. In my lectures I covered the main views, the 'Theistic proofs' and the arguments for and against them. I did not find, however, that I could form any firm view of what I thought religion was about. I got some comfort here from reading C.C.J. Webb, whom I see as one of the wisest of the philosophers of religion. He had collected a number of definitions of religion, and had found that no one of them seemed adequately comprehensive. But he believed that religion would generally be marked by two features, which he called 'ultimacy and intimacy'.[1] It makes a demand which cannot be measured against others (though it can be rejected) and it concerns people in their inner lives. This might be challenged by the sociological theories of religion. Webb looked at these and argued that they were not sufficient.

I was impressed by what he said about 'ultimacy' and 'intimacy', but came to realize that in my case intimacy in an inner religious life went with an ultimate commitment to philosophy. I did not see it quite in those terms at the time. Rather, I saw it as the tension described by William Temple in the Second Chapter of his Gifford Lectures *Nature, Man and God*, where he asks how one can combine the religious attitude of faith in God with the philosophical attitude of open criticism. Both are to be respected; it may be possible to alternate between them. But he was not altogether convincing, or I think, convinced about this. Neither of the two, he says, should assimilate itself 'excessively' to the other. But what is meant by 'excessively'? Temple is on surer ground when he says that both parties should 'respect the principle of Justice – to ta hautou prattein [doing one's own job]. But let no one suppose that this principle is as easy to practice as it is to enunciate.'[2]

I shall come back to this. But first I shall say something about Temple himself. I got to know him personally in the 1930s when he was working on his Gifford Lectures. He wanted to stake out his views in relation to Whitehead's, and he invited me twice to come and stay with him at Bishopthorpe, near York (he was then Archbishop of York) in order to talk to him about Whitehead. The difference was a strong one; Whitehead's God was a logico-aesthetic order for the process of the world, while Temple's was a personal Creator. Temple saw Whitehead soon after the publication of *Nature, Man and God*, when on a visit to Harvard. They evidently met with mutual appreciation. Whitehead said 'Your reasons for disagreeing with me are precisely my reasons for disagreeing with you, so I take it we are really agreed.' Temple told me this with relish on his return. I met him again when he was giving an address to a student conference. He spoke about his faith, and told the students very candidly that he had never had any serious doubt, and that he thought it would have been better if he had. I saw the news of his death in an evening paper when I was getting a train to take a WEA class in a large munitions factory outside Manchester. It was during the War, and Temple was then Archbishop of Canterbury. When I got to my class, I told them this news and spoke of how, with his friend R.H. Tawney he had been one of the founders of the WEA. They were moved. Outwardly, Temple had everything against him for making a popular appeal: sleek and fat with a very upper-class voice, born and bred in the purple in Lambeth Palace. But he became the people's Archbishop: we have not had one since.

To return to how I should now see the tension between philosophy and religion. There are a number of ways in which people try to meet it. Religion (or at any rate theology) is said to be a matter of revelation; or it can be a matter of morality strengthened by stories; or be a purely practical form of life, or purely mystical, or purely aesthetic. The problem is so difficult that I do not think that any serious way of meeting it is to be despised, though I put making it a purely aesthetic matter lowest on my scale. I could not take any of these ways myself, since I thought that in the end both philosophy and religion were concerned (*inter alia*) with truth about how things are. That looked like the need for some metaphysical link, and I had to look at what, in principle, rather than in content, I thought about metaphysics.

It was war-time, and everyone in the University whether professors, lecturers, service staff, students, had to spend one night in six fire-watching in the University Buildings. In the last years of the War there were very few air raid alarms calling us to our stations, and I had to spend long silent hours in an almost empty Arts Building. This was a chance to write, and I wrote much of *The Nature of Metaphysical Thinking* during those times. I looked on metaphysics as a form of analogical thinking. Like Whitehead and Alexander I thought it had to do with general characteristics of reality. But unlike them, I did not think it would be possible to arrive at a unique and all-pervasive set of these, either through Whitehead's method of descriptive generalization or through Alexander's direct discernment. We start from some particular range of experience, and the concepts which could be used to co-ordinate and interpret it, and then we may apply these by analogy to other ranges of experience to see whether they could have an extended use there, and finally, if the resemblances are sufficiently strong to seem significant, we can try to extend the analogy still further to say something about the nature of reality. Thus Hegelian metaphysics makes an extended use of organic concepts; some religious metaphysics of personalist concepts and some materialistic ones of mechanistic concepts.

I am well aware that there are jumps here, especially when I turned from 'co-ordinating' analogies interpreting experience to 'metaphysical' ones which try to say something transcendental. But I think I was right to hold that any such concepts will be drawn from a particular setting, that when used in a different context attention needs to be paid to differences as well as likenesses, and that this is so *a fortiori* if they are used to say something general about 'reality'. I realized that a metaphysician has no privileged access, and that the concepts so selected are unlikely to be fully comprehensive. So any metaphysical view will be partial and provisional. But it starts from concepts used in interpreting experience and comes back to experience in another setting, and so I claimed that the approach could be called empirical in a liberal sense. In this I was attacking any view which makes experience a matter of purely private feelings and sensations. I held it was a matter of interactive responses to what was going on in the environment. I think this was right, but that also I underestimated the power of projections and fantasies.

However, the immediate significance of this far from satisfactory book was that it brought me into contact with other philosophers, and I found that the supposed divide between positivists and metaphysicians was not as deep as it had been thought to be. There was a sense in which we were all just philosophers. I realized this was so at the Joint Session of the Mind Association and the Aristotelian Society, which I organized in Manchester in 1946. Times were still fairly difficult. The students only left the Hall of Residence in the morning and the philosophers arrived in the afternoon. There was very little by way of domestic staff, and the cleanliness left much to be desired. I was embarrassed by this, but I need not have worried. The Hall had an allocation of rations for the students and there were not so many philosophers. So there was plenty of food and people were offered second helpings. In 1946 this was a rare treat, and it made up for any other deficiencies. The following year the Joint Session was held at Trinity College, Cambridge. There meals were more recherché, but also rather sparse, and a hungry philosopher said to me 'In Manchester we had second helpings.'

The 1946 Joint Session was the first real opportunity for philosophers to come together since before the War. There had been some meetings in London in 1945, but these had not been a fully residential house party; people had come in and out to them. So the 1946 Joint Session went with a swing, not only socially but in having some very good papers.[3] R.B. Braithwaite gave his Presidential Address on his theory of Belief and Action. John Wisdom gave his further reflections on 'Other Minds', which he had been pursuing through a series of numbers of *Mind*. There was a symposium 'Why are the calculuses of Logic and Arithmetic applicable to reality?' with Casimir Lewy, Gilbert Ryle and Karl Popper. Popper agreed with Ryle that logical calculuses are rules of inference, procedures for passing from premises to conclusions in reasoning. Arithmetic makes it possible to discover facts about the world, but only as far as the facts and relations in the world can be expressed in the abstractions of the mathematical language. Mathematical languages can be developed which allow the discovery of relations in the world which are not observable. But there are difficulties over the constancy of the relations in the world which may not continue the same over time. In the discussion, Popper said 'If you put two balls together in a bag, you are sure you will get two out. You put two rabbits together and you are not sure you will get only two.' Someone said 'But then something has happened', and Popper said 'In reality something always happens.'

The last time I heard Popper speak was some years ago when Professor Michael Redhead invited him to Cambridge to address the seminar in the History and Philosophy of Science. Thinking this would need a larger room than the usual one, he took the Lady Mitchell Hall, the biggest lecture theatre in the University, fearing however that it might be very far from full. In the event it was packed with an audience of about 500. Popper remarked 'Professor Redhead invited me to his seminar: you seem to have rather large seminars in Cambridge.' He then said that Professor Redhead in his introduction had mentioned his political philosophy. 'I am not a political philosopher, but I have a political philosophy which can be put in two sentences, and, as I see a number of young people around me, I will give it. This is a wonderful world. The intellectuals will tell you that it is hell, but you must not believe them.' He then went on to speak about the main conclusion he had come to in a long life spent doing the philosophy of science. It was that we live in an open world of propensities and not in a closed deterministic system. I found his manner of putting this moving as well as persuasive.

I had a personal encounter with Popper when he came to this country from New Zealand after the War and had just published *The Open Society and its Enemies* (London, Routledge, 1945). I had reviewed it, and while applauding it in general, I challenged his saying that not only was Plato a Fascist, but that teaching students Plato's *Republic* turned them into young Fascists. I said that, as one who had been introduced to Philosophy through the *Republic*, I had not found this was so. We did not believe in philosopher kings nor in the separate classes. Rather, reading the *Republic* gave us talking points. I also drew attention to the intemperance of his attack on Hegel. Popper came to give a lecture in Manchester and I was to put him up for the night. When I went up to him and introduced myself after the lecture he launched into an attack on me for the review. There was then a dinner with colleagues and he had to break off.

Afterwards when we went to my house he started again. I told him that I thought he spoilt his case by overstatement; he said he thought that if he put things in an extreme way people would believe at any rate part of what he was saying. As he had only recently come to this country, I took the liberty of telling him that I did not think he would find that this worked in England. Confronted by overstatement we tended to think of what could be said on the other side. I was no Hegelian, but the violence of his attack had made me think that this could not be the whole picture. He said 'Do you really think that is so in England?' I do not know how far, if at all, this later influenced his manner of criticism. He then continued to attack me until, at about midnight, being very tired, I suggested we should retire. Whereupon he completely changed his manner. He said 'I feel better now I have said all that to you', and he became gentle and rather affectionate. Whenever I met him subsequently he was gentle and affectionate. A good row can be a bond.

There was another notable Joint Session in 1948. This was held in Trinity College, Dublin, and combined with a celebration of Berkeley's bicentenary, so that most of the papers were on Berkeley. One on Berkeley as a mathematician was given by De Valera who was Taosaoch at the time, and had previously been a lecturer in Mathematics at the University College. I stayed with a Dublin friend, Lionel Booth, who was a deputy in the Dail in De Valera's party, Fianna Fáil. De Valera was about to face a vote of censure, and my friend asked his secretary whether he was worried about it. 'Not he. He has only talked about Berkeley for a week.' Those were happier days for Irish politicians. The Joint Session was presided over by H.C. Luce, the Provost of Trinity, who had edited Berkeley's *Commonplace Book*. He had been a colonel in the Black and Tans during the Troubles of the early 1920s and De Valera had been in prison. Now they sat next to each other in the front row (perhaps talking about Berkeley). Someone told Luce that I was a kinswoman of Robert Emmet, a darling of the Irish people who was hanged for his part in the abortive rising of 1805. Our family had a connection, but we are not able to trace it. Luce told me he must introduce me to the Taosaoch, who was very affable and told me I should go and look at the Emmet house outside Dublin, which I did. People in Ireland will sometimes say to me 'Then you must be Irish', and I say not; the Emmets were originally English and I am from the branch which stayed in England, whereas Robert Emmet's family had gone to

Ireland and he was a radical member of the Protestant Ascendency. This is not so welcome.

There is a sequel to this. Robert Emmet's brother, Dr Thomas Addis Emmet, emigrated to New York and founded a family whose descendants still flourish. I was in New York as a Visiting Professor at Columbia and Barnard Colleges, and was seeing H.J. Paton, the Kantian scholar and former Professor of Philosophy at St Andrew's. He was staying with his daughter, who was married to a New York surgeon, and they lived in West Chester, up the Hudson River where the very rich commute from beautiful houses. Paton told people there that he had been seeing Dorothy Emmet, a kinswoman of Robert Emmet. One of them was a descendant of Thomas Addis Emmet. So I was invited to go out to dinner and spend the night. I was driven out by one of their number, a Wall Street banker. At dinner they called me 'cousin', although there was no real connection. Our host, a stockbroker whose wife was the Emmet, started cross-questioning me on what I was lecturing about. They thought it very odd; I got some support from Paton, who said: 'You know, that is the sort of thing we talk about.' Finally, my host the stockbroker said 'Do they pay you to talk about this?' I said, 'Extraordinarily enough, they do', and he said 'Then I suppose it is all right.' Was Philosophy being put in its place?

MICHAEL POLANYI

Philosophy was put in a very different place by my Manchester colleague, Michael Polanyi. Polanyi was a Hungarian Jew who came to Manchester as a refugee in the 1930s from the Kaiser Wilhelm Institute in Berlin. He was a physical chemist who was doing distinguished work especially on crystalline solutions at high temperatures. I am not competent to speak about this work. Any interested will find some account, by his son John Polanyi, with a bibliography of his scientific papers, in *The Logic of Personal Knowledge*.[4] However, his scientific interests ceased to be central. He was preoccupied by the threats to science which he saw coming on the one hand from encroaching Marxism and on the other hand from positivism in philosophy as he saw it. His thinking moved first into economics and then into social philosophy where he was working at a view of the nature of science as dependent on a society which gave it moral support. As his heart was no longer in the Department of

Chemistry, nor indeed in the particular work of any department, the University Senate offered him a personal chair in which he could follow his concerns. As it was not easy to predict how these might develop, the chair was called 'Social Studies', a title thought sufficiently general to admit of his following his interests into whatever field they might lead him without departmental responsibilities. His distinction was such as to justify this free position, and in those happy days there was money to support it.

In 1951 Polanyi gave the Gifford Lectures in the University of Aberdeen. These were developed into a large book *Personal Knowledge* (London, Routledge, 1958). It contains a sustained polemic against views that knowledge can be depersonalized, either in analytic techniques in philosophy or in the critical and experimental techniques in science. There is always the personal element, the claim of a knower that what he says is true: this is called 'the fiduciary mode'. There is clearly a problem over objectivity. Polanyi insists that he is no subjectivist. The truth claim is made by a person following clues while in rapport with reality – producing, of course, a further problem over the nature of the rapport. Polanyi attacks the correspondence theory, and indeed taken as meaning that propositions and the world can be matched, this is only too open to attack. Yet there is a difference between realism which looks to an external world for reference, and any view which makes knowledge a purely internal matter. Polanyi wants to be on the side of the realists, but his fiduciary mode seems to produce an internal view of truth. He says that to say a sentence is true is to authorize its assertion, so that truth becomes not a property of a proposition p, but the rightness of an action in which a speaker accredits his belief that p. This could be a form of the redundancy theory of truth. Polanyi refers with approval to P.F. Strawson's one-time version of this, when to say 'p is true' is like putting your hand on your heart when you say 'p'. But if to say 'p is true' is to say 'I believe p', there is a problem over error and corrigibility. If truth is the rightness of the action of believing p, there is a problem analogous to the one which worried Prichard over the rightness of the act of doing one's duty – is this the subjective duty to do what I believe to be right or the objective duty to do what would really be right though I don't know what it is? Prichard had regretfully come down on the side of my duty to do what I subjectively believe is right. The dilemma is stronger in the case of asserting what I believe to be true, since this is a matter of cognition and it might be argued that morality is non-cognitive. The parallel is that I could be right to believe that p, given the reasons and evidence available to me, and yet I could be wrong in fact. Polanyi allows that we can come to change our sincere beliefs: this could surely only be denied by a fanatic. So it is now right for me to say that I no longer believe p, though there was a time when it was right for me to say that I believed p. I mentioned reasons and evidence. Polanyi presses the fiduciary mode at every point; reasons and evidence only have a role in my beliefs because I assent to them.

The difficulty I find here might have been alleviated if Polanyi had known J.L. Austin's distinction between the locutionary and the illocutionary forces of utterances.[5] The former is something with a certain meaning and reference. The latter is some act of a particular kind done in uttering it, for instance warning or ordering. In Polanyi's case, the illocutionary act might be called 'avowing'. He fastens on the illocutionary force – any sentence is or could be asserted by a speaker who is carrying out a speech act in asserting it as true, and so he or she believes it. This is to accept Moore's paradox, that one cannot say 'I know p is true but I do not believe p.' Logically, Moore was probably right, but I think that it may be possible to get into this position psychologically. At any rate, there is the difference between what Cardinal Newman in *The Grammar of Assent* called 'notional' and 'real assent'. For Polanyi all assent should be real assent, 'accredited' by a personal act of commitment. I think, however, there is an ambiguity in his concept of 'commitment'. Commitment to what? One can be committed to seeking truth, and in doing so to admitting that one's beliefs are corrigible, so that commitment to the truth of a particular belief does not have the same irreversible quality that attaches to the commitment to truth itself. I came to appreciate this distinction more clearly in writing my recent book, *The Role of the Unrealisable*.[6] Truth (with a capital T) I take to be a Regulative Ideal; setting an orientation to our practical reason. Truth as a Regulative Ideal is not instantiable in any set of particular truths. These are truths with a little t, where 'truth' can be a property of propositions which can be true or false, whether or not we know which they are. We follow such clues as we can in trying to find out. But this means disengaging the locutionary aspect of what the proposition asserts from the illocutionary aspect of making the assertion. Certainly it may be very difficult to see what is being asserted – hence all the discussions which go on over the meaning of what is being said. This is a critical activity, guided by the conviction that what is true is not necessarily what we are sincerely asserting, and that we may have to be prepared to correct cherished beliefs.

This means detaching the little t's of propositions from the big T of ultimate commitment, and it may be that commitment to the big T may be needed to safeguard the little t's, the truths which do not depend on our convictions as to what we believe.[7]

Polanyi cared passionately about commitment to Truth with the big T. I doubt whether he struggled much with the difference between this and our often properly provisional commitment to the particular little t's. In consequence in spite of his concern for rapport with reality his view of knowledge tends towards an internalist one of warranted assertibility, where (as he says at times) the 'warrant' is provided by the assertion itself as an act of personal commitment.

In combining truth, assertion and commitment Polanyi was in fact drawing attention to the tension between faith and criticism about which I spoke earlier in this chapter. I do not think he resolved this – if it is resolvable – but this was because he was firmly on the side of faith. This could lead to a manner of preaching rather than arguing, and also to a stereotyped and simplified version of the views which he was attacking. I mention this as it is an attitude which can be found in some of his followers, more strongly indeed than in Polanyi himself who used to say to me 'Keep on with your criticism.' It hinders their effective engagement with other philosophers.

Yet I do not want to end on a note of criticism. I have great admiration for much that Polanyi said and wrote. In particular there is his view of tacit knowledge, the penumbra surrounding whatever we hold in focal awareness; how this enriches thinking, and how what is tacit can be made focal, or what is focal dismissed into the background. There is also the wealth of illustration in reports of actual processes of discovery, where the personal factor is clearly present. *Personal Knowledge* could be read, if for nothing else, as a study in heuristics, akin in some ways to Arthur Koestler's *Act of Creation*, but richer, written by one who was himself more deeply immersed in scientific discovery. Finally, he was a good friend of the Department of Philosophy, and a very dear personal friend and colleague. On one occasion during the War, when rationing was tight, I happened to have two chops. It was a Sunday, and I knew Michael was alone, so I rang him up and asked him if he would like to come and eat one of them. He said 'Can I really? I want to speak to you anyway. I want to ask you if I can dedicate my new book to you.' (It was three lectures, *Science, Faith and Society* (Oxford University Press, London and New York, 1946).) 'But I'd thought of doing this, before you said you would cook me a chop.' That was worth several chops.

9

Philosophy in Manchester: Theories in the Social Sciences. Alasdair MacIntyre, Max Gluckman

I became head of the Philosophy Department in Manchester just after the War, when Professor A.D. Ritchie went to Edinburgh. I had one colleague, A.E. Teale, and my former place was not filled at once. Ex-servicemen were pouring back, and we had very large classes. We got a third member, Wolfe Mays, and I asked him to take the Intermediate Logic course. Intermediate Latin had been compulsory for most Arts degrees. Ex-servicemen had forgotten their school Latin and were given exemption. The Dean of the Faculty remarked as an *obiter dictum* that they should do something with some stiffening such as Logic. Mays used to come out of the Intermediate Logic class covered in chalk after struggling over exercises on the blackboard with about a hundred ex-service students. It was a strenuous time, but a good one. There was none of the estrangement one hears about between civilians and those that had been in the armed forces in the First World War, perhaps because we had all been involved to some extent. Also there had not been the traumatic segregation of the trenches.

I had authority for an Assistant Lecturer in Political Theory. One of the applicants was a young man just out of the forces, Roy Jenkins. We called him for interview but after an amicable discussion both sides decided that it was not his job. In his autobiography he speaks gratefully of this, as having made him realize that he did not want to be a university teacher. Politics in this country might have been the poorer if he had become my assistant.

ALASDAIR MACINTYRE

The ablest student I had at that time, or probably at any time, was Alasdair MacIntyre. He had been exempt from military service on health grounds and had done a degree in Classics in the University of London. He came to Manchester to do a post-graduate degree in Philosophy and stayed on as an assistant lecturer. At that time he was a Presbyterian and a candidate for a minister in the Church of Scotland, having been a member of the Communist Party while in London. When a Presbyterian, he held Barthian neo-orthodox views in Theology. Subsequently he became an atheist, and he is now a Roman Catholic. I found these changes disconcerting but came to think that there was a connecting thread running through them – an opposition to liberalism. He saw liberalism in all its forms as concerned with individuals pursuing their interests and as lacking in roots. (I do not agree with this, but that is another story.)

I made contact with Alasdair again in the 1960s, when I had come to live in Cambridge and he was a Professor in the University of Essex. We had both developed strong interests in theories in the Social Sciences and in the philosophical questions that come up in the course of that work. We decided that there was a place for a book collecting together important articles which illustrated the latter in particular. We were not concerned with an overall theory of the Social Sciences, still less with recommending an overall philosophical view. We were looking for writings by sociologists and anthropologists of a high level of sophistication who used philosophical concepts in their work, and we tried to show how these were related to the empirical aspects. Alasdair selected six articles by sociologists, I selected six by anthropologists, and we wrote a joint Introduction. We found that we had no difficulty in agreeing on what we wanted to say. The book was called *Sociological Theory and Philosophical Analysis*;[1] it came out at a time when courses in Sociology were proliferating, and there was a demand for discussions of their theoretical implications. The book was translated into Japanese.[2]

This was a time when Alasdair and I could be in close touch both intellectually and geographically. He later went to America; our contact now is through occasional, but also warm, correspondence. His three big books (all published by Duckworth, London), *After Virtue* (1981), *Whose Justice, Which Rationality?* (1988) and *Three Rival Versions of Moral Enquiry* (1990) are a sustained attack on the abstract nature of contemporary moral theory, claiming that conceptions of morality and practical reason emerge within particular kinds of social order which themselves embody conceptual traditions. This may sound like the sociology of knowledge, but it is more subtle than what usually passes under that title, when philosophical theories are said to be dependent on pre-conceptual interests and needs. In his view the forms of social life are partly at least shaped by the concepts for which they provide a context. Nor is it a simple relativism; rather, it is a dialectical view in which concepts change not only in response to social pressures, but to the internal intellectual development of the tradition in which they occur. Above all, a tradition, if it is to be a living tradition, needs to have creative intellectual resources to meet critical attacks from followers of other traditions. Followers of traditions need not – or should not – simply preach at each other from their respective soap boxes. A creative tradition can incorporate elements from other traditions; he holds that mediaeval Thomism was able to incorporate Augustinian as well as Aristotelian elements. Thomism is the tradition which gets highest marks. Mediaeval historians can tell us how far Thomist principles of worldly dominion under moral and theological sanctions informed social and political institutions; *pace* Dante's *De Monarchia*, I wonder whether in fact they did so. This is of more than historical interest, since MacIntyre looks to a re-thought Thomism as the best philosophical hope for our fragmented society. He knows that a tradition cannot be produced to order. He looks rather for forms of community, probably out of the mainstream, within which a tradition can be nurtured.

> What matters at this stage is the construction of local forms of community within which civility and the intellectual and moral life can be sustained through the new dark ages which are already upon us. And if the tradition of the virtues was able to survive the horrors of the last dark ages, we are not entirely without grounds for hope. This time however the barbarians are not waiting beyond the frontiers; they have already been governing us for quite some time. And it is our lack of consciousness of this that constitutes part of our predicament. We are waiting not for a Godot, but for another – doubtless very different – St. Benedict.[3]

Intellectually a revitalized Thomism would have to meet what MacIntyre describes as the Humean critique of reason and morality.

My acquaintance with contemporary Thomism is all too slight. I am aware of a considerable philosophical world going on in its own milieu in virtual isolation from most analytic philosophy. MacIntyre knows analytic philosophy from within. If he can bring its critical methods to bear on contemporary Thomism, it may be possible for others of us to come closer to it. It may also be possible for Thomists to test the resources of their philosophy to meet the demands of a very different intellectual climate from that in which their tradition was formed. For instance, its teleology was that of a world in which things developed towards fulfilling their essential natures; can this be re-thought for a world which, scientifically, is one of energy and mathematical laws, and which, philosophically, if it contains teleological processes will probably need to see these as less streamlined and more open than those of the Thomist, Aristotelian world?

I am sure that MacIntyre does not underestimate the difficulty of reconstructing a Thomist form of philosophy in a climate which is both socially and intellectually non-Thomist. It will no doubt be necessary to translate the language of 'Being', which now seems strange to us. Heidegger tried to do something of the kind, but he seems to lose sight of *Sein* in a kaleidoscopic world of *Dasein*, of what is contingently *there*. Nor had he assimilated analytic philosophy.

My main intellectual concern in the 1950s and 1960s was in the philosophy of the Social Sciences. I had come nearer to appreciating the importance of analytic methods, but I had also come to think that these were most profitably used by philosophers who were also interested in something besides philosophy itself, some subject matter which throws up linguistic and conceptual problems and where philosophers might be able to get in on the act with the practitioners. My role model was Herbert Hart, who had been trained in the Law before coming into philosophy, and who was to become Professor of Jurisprudence in Oxford after being a philosophy don. No one to my knowledge has done more to clear up conceptual confusions over questions such as the nature of rights, sovereignty, natural law. His book *The Concept of Law* (Oxford, Clarendon Press, 1961) is something of a minor classic, dealing mainly with the nature of a legal system. I have called him a role model; I do not mean that I could hope to approximate to this model, since I have no comparable subject outside philosophy; my increasingly rusty knowledge of the Classics hardly counts, and its main help has been to sharpen my feeling for the meanings of words, and of course to bring me to Plato and Aristotle in Greek. So I needed another subject-matter to get my teeth into.

It came with my increasing interest in Anthropology. This started in Oxford, when I attended R.R. Marett's lectures on Primitive Morals. R.R. Marett was a philosopher turned anthropologist, and a considerable character. I still get pleasure from talking about him with his Australian grandson, the philosopher David Armstrong whose mother, Marett's daughter, had married an Australian naval officer. David Armstrong told me that, while his grandfather had no racial sense, he had considerable class sense, and always wanted to talk to the Chief. I said 'As one Seigneur to another', and David said, 'Precisely' (Marett held a Seigneurie in Jersey).

MAX GLUCKMAN

Marett was helping to found the subject as it is now, or rather, as it was to become after the War. In Manchester we acquired our first Professor of Social Anthropology, Max Gluckman, a South African, who had been at Exeter College, Oxford, where he knew Marett well. He had done detailed field work at the Rhodes-Livingstone Institute in what was then Northern Rhodesia. His book *The Judicial Process among the Barotse of Northern Rhodesia* came out in 1955 (Manchester, Manchester University Press). Max had had a legal training before he turned to Anthropology; and the book can also be read with an interest in the nature of a legal system, in this case in a pre-literate culture. He sees it as a set of rules 'concerning what ought to be done', and therefore as continuous with morality. The guiding notion is that there are reasonable ways of acting in accordance with custom; both 'reasonable' and 'customary' being concepts which are flexible enough for use in differing situations. Indeed, the book can be taken as illustrating the need to combine 'the certainty of law' with 'the uncertainty of legal concepts', showing that a degree of ambiguity can be a strength and not a weakness in a legal system.[4] The book contains Gluckman's recordings of a number of trials, some with alluring titles such as 'The Case of the Official Wrongdoers', and 'The Case of the Man who helped his Mother-in-Law cross a Ford'. There is no sharp distinction between legal rules and moral practices, and the judgments contain a good deal of shrewd advice on how to behave.

I have drawn attention to the book to illustrate how I was entering a world of my anthropology colleagues which could be full of interest for a philosopher. Moreover, I found my taking part in their seminars was welcomed and I was not looked on as an outsider who had never done any field work. They knew I was genuinely interested. Indeed, Victor Turner, in a Foreword to the Second Edition of my *Function, Purpose and Powers*, calls me 'our friendly neighbourhood philosopher'. Victor Turner was one of the most gifted members of a gifted and growing department of Social Anthropology. My association with anthropologists also taught me to drink beer in pubs. At six o' clock sharp, when the pub opened, the seminar would close officially and we repaired to the College Arms across the road, where the discussion would continue indefinitely.

As a social anthropologist coming from South Africa, Max saw attendance at soccer matches as a form of British folk religion, and one in which he was glad to participate. As the big chief in his Department he pressed his members of staff to do so too. I joined them for a match, and the next week he rang me up. 'Dorothy, we will expect you at 2 p.m. at London Road Station on Saturday to get the train to _____'. He took a poor view when he found my attendance had been a one-off. The 1950s were the best time I have known for doing philosophy in an interdisciplinary setting. The University had grown rapidly, and besides undergraduates we had a number of graduate students, particularly in the Faculty of Economic and Social Studies, who wanted to bring Philosophy into their work. Max Gluckman in Anthropology, Bill Mackenzie in Government, Ely Devons in Economics and myself in Philosophy formed something of a quartet. We talked to each other as well as sharing seminars. Bill Mackenzie has testified to this intellectual friendship in his Preface to his *Politics and Social Science* (Penguin, 1967); this book reads in parts like a series of reflections on our discussions, which, he says, were 'held in various environments, some of them not very academic'. One was, of course, the College Arms. Max and Ely have now died. I am still in touch with Bill Mackenzie, and I think gratefully of our collaboration in the Political Philosophy courses; of his common sense, and his capacity to think of unlikely sources of likely enlightenment. (Anyone interested in what these might be could consult the Book List in *Politics and Social Science*.)

FUNCTIONS AND ROLES

My book, *Function, Purpose and Powers*[5] came out of all this. The dominant social theory of that time was 'functionalism', and one of its main exponents, Radcliffe Brown, was visiting us in Manchester as a Simon Professor. (Lord Simon of Wythenshawe gave the University a handsome endowment for Visiting Professors and Research Fellows.) 'Functionalism' was sharpened by Radcliffe Brown after its launch by Malinowski. It was a method of looking for explanations of social activities in terms of how they helped to maintain a present structure of social relations, and not in terms of historical origins or psychological motivations. Radcliffe Brown wrote 'the function of any recurrent activity such as the punishment of a crime, or a funeral ceremony' is 'the part which it plays in the social life as a whole and therefore the contribution it makes to the social maintenance of the structural community'.[6]

I was uneasy about Functionalism on various counts. For one, it did not seem to distinguish between the reasons why people carried out an activity and its unintended but socially beneficient effects. These consequences may not be the reasons why the activity is carried out. This was in effect one of the things Marx was saying; I have said to students that they can try forgetting about the Dialectic and read Marx as a pioneer of structural sociology. The study of unintended consequences of social activities seemed, and still seems, to me to be one of the most important themes in sociology.

Robert Merton went some way in distinguishing between 'manifest' and 'latent' functions, borrowing these terms from Freudian analysts.[7] But, as with the Freudians, the 'latent' function not consciously intended, and not the 'manifest' intended one, gets to be seen as the *real* reason for the activity. This is so in particular if a latent function is given as an *explanation*. Where a manifest function, as purposively intended, is accepted as an explanation, this can be a teleological one in a straightforward sense. Where the latent function and the contribution made to maintaining the social structure is given as an explanation, this would be covertly teleological. There is an analogy, welcomed by functional sociologists, with the integrated activities in biological organisms. The covert teleology still plagues biologists. That is their problem; and here I am concerned with the problem for the sociologists. The term 'function' is used to speak of how different activities supplement, counteract, or sustain one another in the ongoing process of the life of the organism. So it is said that the function of the heart is to circulate the blood, and correspondingly the flow of blood through the heart enables it to go on beating. One activity has a influence on another with effect on its next stage; so there is a feed-back loop. But 'functional explanation' can be a misleading expression. The right expression should be 'structural-functional', and here it is the '*structural*' side of the partnership which is explanatory, and the 'functional' side is heuristic, calling attention to an effect to be explained. The explanation can be looked for in the structural relations between the constituents of the system, in the sociological case these being persons in institutional settings. I don't think I saw this clearly enough when I wrote my *Function, Purpose and Powers*; I still spoke, even though critically, about 'functional explanations'. That the causal explanation lay in the structural relations between the participants in a co-ordinated activity, while the functional effects drew attention to the need for explanation, was something that came to me one day in the library of Columbia University, where I was on a visit. I rang up Robert Merton, who said 'Go and write that down at once.' So I did.

To return to Radcliffe Brown's example of the funeral ceremony. His 'functional explanation' might be that of an agnostic professor who finds it appropriate to attend a colleague's religious funeral, while dismissing as much as possible what is being said by those who believe that they are commending their friend to God. This kind of situation is now so familiar that we hardly realize how a latent function is parasitic on a manifest purpose. But the function of strengthening ties between the bereaved and helping them to face the next stage of their lives is not likely to have this effect except where there are structural ties already present between family and friends. Otherwise, the ceremony may just be a *rite-de-passage*, a way of closing a chapter, though this itself is no mean function. And it can be more than this, even when taken functionally. I once went to a colleague's funeral with Max Gluckman; there was a Vaughan Williams anthem containing the words 'See that ye love one another with a pure heart fervently.' When we came out Max said, 'It is wonderful to come together and hear those words; what a pity someone has to die for it to happen.' People might say that he could hear this, or something like it, at some other service; there need not be a funeral. But anthropologists generally think of religion in terms of ritual, and of ritual as significant when carried out by people who are living and working together in other contexts. In these days a funeral may well be one of the few such occasions for this to happen.

Another reason for dissatisfaction with the functional sociology I met in the 1950s was that the analogy with a biological organism presented societies as too closely integrated. This may have seemed plausible in that the method was primarily being used by anthropologists studying pre-literate 'primitive' societies, which were certainly more close-knit that our 'modern' ones. But even there, I had my doubts over the term 'the Social System', which had been put into general use by Talcott Parsons. I attacked the notion by claiming that a society was a process with some systematic characteristics rather than a system, and since the participants in the process are persons, they may have purposive motivations for their activities. Moreover, persons are related in more than one way, and their purposive interactions in one activity may have unintended consequences in others. Sociologists and anthropologists are very properly interested in these repercussions and where these are unintended, motivation can be ignored. But political philosophers (and I was one) are properly interested in policy-making and governmental action where an attempt, even if unsuccessful, is made to give some direction to some of these activities. Functional sociologists would try to show how, when conflicts arise, these may be met by countervailing tendencies within the 'system'. I realized that a good deal of political theory in the past had been written largely, if not exclusively, in the language of Purpose. My associations with the social scientists had made me more aware of how structural characteristics in social relations can limit, or counteract, what is being attempted purposively. I was also aware that effectiveness in producing social change could sometimes be due to individuals of exceptional ability. I was not advocating a 'great man' view of history; exceptional individuals would need to be in the right place at the right time. Also their innovations needed to find some institutional embodiment if they were to make a lasting contribution. Otherwise we have interesting biographies, but social processes may revert pretty much to their former patterns. I took as one of my examples Florence Nightingale, who was not only the gentle 'Lady with the Lamp', but an upper-class young woman of great ability, who could use her social influence in high places to get herself and her associates out to the Crimea with resources to do something about the appalling state of the military hospitals. Her lasting contribution was to change the nurse's role from its Sarah Gamp image to that of a professionally trained woman – a role which now has the Royal College of Nursing behind it. In later life she became an invalid, possibly a *malade imaginaire*, taking to her bed and thereby escaping the social round in which she would have been expected to take part. She carried on extensive studies into matters affecting the care of the sick not only in this country, and she was particularly aware of the importance of sanitary conditions. She became a self-taught accomplished statistician and used statistics as a weapon of presentation. The economist the late Professor Sir Richard Stone has devoted a chapter to her in a forthcoming book on the pioneers of statistics.[8]

She can therefore be taken as an instance of the combination of the three factors, 'Function', 'Purpose', and 'Powers'. 'Function' stands for an activity as fulfilling a social need in relation to others; 'Purpose' stands for a deliberate effort to do something about a perceived need; and 'Powers' is the word I chose for the creative abilities of individuals.[9]

The key concept in all this is that of a person in a 'role', carrying out a function in an institutional setting; what he or she is trying to accomplish through this; and the particular way in which he or she carries it out. I had been saying something to this effect to Robert Merton's seminar while on the visit to Columbia University in 1960 to which I have already referred. After the seminar Merton took me into his office, became very solemn, and said I must write a book on this. The result was my *Roles, Rules and Relations* (London, 1966). The book owes a great deal to discussions with Robert Merton. I returned to Columbia in 1962 when I had taken up his suggestion and was working it out. I was also working it out in the period of student revolts, when 'soul-less' had become almost an inseparable epithet of 'bureaucrat' as applied to those running the universities, and when 'existentialism' was in fashion as a view that free actions should be the disengaged actions of lonely individuals. In the Preface to my book I said that if I had not dedicated it (as I did) to my friends at Columbia University, I should have liked to dedicate it 'to administrators whose hearts are with the anarchists, and anarchists who can have a heart for the administrators'.

Existentialism was in effect an anarchist morality. Action in a role, and still more, following a prescribed code, was slave morality. (I had heard something like this before from John Macmurray, with reference to duty and obligation.) Authentic action was the outcome of an individual's personal decision; to follow the expectations of how one should behave in a role was at best play-acting, more probably insincere *mauvaise foi*. Sartre's description of the waiter has often been quoted. 'His movement is quick and forward, a little too precise, a little too rapid. He comes towards the patrons with a step a little too quick. He bends forward a little too eagerly; his voice, his eyes, express an interest a little too solicitous for the order of the customer.'[10] Sartre says he is playing at being a waiter, and that the same will apply to a grocer, a tailor, an auctioneer, trying to persuade their clientele that they are nothing but a grocer, a tailor, an auctioneer, and that this is what society demands. The role of the waiter is of course a particularly stylized one; less so that of the grocer. And there may be a moment of personal communication between grocer and customer; the customer has heard that the grocer's wife is ill, and he does not just exchange a conventional remark about the weather.

But I was not only interested in how players of roles can behave as persons in off moments. I was concerned with the presence of the person in the *persona*. A *persona* was originally the mask through which the actor of a role in a play spoke his part. Nowadays masks have been discarded. The actor in a role is a person playing it with individual style. And outside the theatre 'one man in his time plays many parts'; he need not be enclosed in any one of them. This was brought home to me when the philosopher Paul Tillich was in my house. I had a rather aristocratic German girl staying with me, and she had married a local bus driver. She and Tillich, both Germans, got into a confidential conversation; she was saying that she could not tell her parents because 'my husband is only a bus driver'. He said 'Your husband is a bus driver, but he is not *only* a bus driver.' Indeed, he was not; but even with a less distinctive character than this man had, there is always the person in the *persona*, making judgements and adjustments that will be needed if a role is not to be an impractical stereotype.

However, I was not only concerning myself with the need to recognize that there is a person in the *persona*, but also with the person's own need for roles in which he or she knows more or less what is expected and indeed what they should expect from themselves. Otherwise one might say with Wordsworth 'me this unchartered freedom tires', and this, *pace* the Existentialists, would not just be because we were too weak to be ourselves.

My concern for the need for a person in the roles and for roles in which one can live as a person brought me another philosophical friend besides Robert Merton. This was Sir Geoffrey Vickers, who wrote to me about *Rules, Roles and Relations* and invited me to stay with him. He had been a young subaltern in the First World War, and had been awarded the VC for holding an outpost, I believe virtually single-handed, until he was finally relieved. He told me that the Germans were throwing hand grenades at him, and, as a cricketer, he fielded each as it came and threw it back. So he certainly could act in an individual capacity. For most of his life subsequently he was a bureaucratic lawyer and certainly no 'soul-less' one. Finally, he was in charge of recruitment, health, welfare and training on the National Coal Board. His letter to me went deeply into the necessity for roles so I give it more or less in full.

Dear Professor Emmet,
I have just been re-reading Rules, Roles and Relations and one purpose of this letter is to thank you for all I have profited from it and other writings of yours.

The other purpose is to offer you, very diffidently, a thought which is probably not new to you, though it only occurred to me after re-reading your chapter on persons and personae. It seems to me that in considering how far a person is more than a bundle of roles, one must distinguish the viewpoint of the role-player from that of those who rely on the role.

The latter, judging the performance of their doctor, employer or what not, can appeal to a socially set standard of what is to be expected of the player of such a role. But within this set of expectations there is another, generated by the past performance of the role-player. They might complain – 'Though what you have done is not outside the range of what my society expects from *any* doctor, employer, father, etc. it is *not like you*'.

Roles vary in the discretion they leave to the player; but this discretion is further structured by the performance of the player himself, who invites others to base their expectations on his particular performance and creates the standards by which his own discretions are to be judged.

At the extreme of discretion is the role of 'being me'. Though no social norm insists that I shall be one sort of acceptable person, rather than another, I myself, in so far as I become a coherent personality, invite others to rely on the 'person' that I am becoming and invite the complaint – 'that is not like you', if I let them down by this, my self-designated standard.

Other people, however, can distinguish between those expectations of me which are socially attached to the roles I play and those which my own playing has invited them to form.

From my own point of view, on the other hand, this distinction is nothing like so clear. The social expectations attached to my manifold roles, as father, husband, lawyer and so on are for me self-expectations in so far as I have accepted them, and I cannot distinguish these self-expectations from those which have grown up within the discretions which society allows me. For me, it is not limiting to describe myself as a bundle of roles but as a comprehensive role or person, which subsumes my version of a whole series of personae.

Of course, I am not in fact so coherent as that (even at the end of a long life) and am constantly letting other people and myself down. I also have a status, as a person, to criticise the social expectations attached to various roles, whether played by myself or others. I may even feel the need to get martyred in the course of trying to change them. But what I cannot conceivably do is the existentialist's inversion, in wanting to be unpredictable in order to be more fully myself.

I have found very helpful your discussion of the existentialist case in this book but you don't fully uncover what seems to me to be its basic irrationality. If as I conceive it, the activity of living consists basically in building a coherent, unique persona out of the bundle of inconsistent possibilities in the pram, then why should living in a socially structured world make existentialists want to be untrustworthy even to their fellow rebels. Those who can't find room to develop their persons within the discretions allowed by their society in any of its sub-cultures, can find it in rebellion or anarchy; but this involves building trustworthy expectations between self and fellow rebels, fellow anarchists.

I welcomed the support I got from Sir Geoffrey over the pervasiveness, but not I think all-pervasiveness, of roles, and over the scope they give for personal discretion. I am not sure whether I can go as far as he did in thinking of a role of being myself, or being a particular kind of person who tries not to let down other people's and my own expectations of my ways of behaving. To make being myself a role seems to put another *persona* inside the *personae*; *persona* seems to require a degree of general description. Being a particular kind of human being might be such a description, but would the *persona* filling this role then just be me? To give myself a central role in being myself seems to call for too much self-consciousness over my behaviour. But I was completely with Sir Geoffrey in attacking the existentialist's claim that the individual person is only free when making decisions outside roles, and roles are stereotypes. They may indeed become stereotypes, but they also admit creative discretion – which is as well, since most action in human relations will be action in roles.

I also found myself in sympathy with Sir Geoffrey over his views on policy-making and negotiations. He had written about ways of moving to collective decisions in his *The Art of Judgement* (London, 1965) and *Freedom in a Rocking Boat* (London, 1970), and had been engaged in a number of negotiations in the course of his life. He attacked the notion that rational procedures consist in finding efficient means to pre-envisaged ends, or else bargaining from fixed positions. In a negotiation the purpose may change through the process of trying to see what should be done. The emphasis should be on a process, and realizing that a process of deliberation can affect the attitudes and ideas of those engaged in it and set their aims in a different light. One of his examples was the Report of the Royal Commission on Capital Punishment (the Gower Report of 1949).[11] This commission was set up by the Government of the day in face of a growing movement for abolition to consider and report whether liability under the criminal law in Great Britain to impose capital punishment should be limited or modified and to what extent and by what means. Its terms of reference therefore excluded a recommendation for abolition, and the recommendations it put forward for giving a jury discretion to find 'degrees' of homicide through diminished responsibility or other extenuating circumstances in fact showed there was no satisfactory halfway house between the existing state of affairs and the abolition of the death penalty. So the result of the deliberations of the Commission was to strengthen the movement for abolition which it had been set up to counter.

This is an extreme example of Sir Geoffrey's general insistence that the original ends for a deliberation, if it is to be fruitful, may be modified as the deliberation proceeds. In this case deliberation was not fruitful since modification was not envisaged.

There is a similar view that negotiations and decision-making should be seen as *processes* in Chester Barnard's book *The Functions of the Executive*.[12] Chester Barnard was president of the New Jersey Bell Telephone Company. He had been a member of the Harvard

Society of Fellows in the 1930s where he used to discuss these matters with Whitehead, and I can catch Whiteheadian echoes in his book. Writing about decision-making in organizations, he says that while a decision should be definite, it is vital to realize that it will be likely to have been made under imperfect information, in a perspective in which factors in the environment – personal, economic, political, geographic, and others – are perceived through limitations in those perceiving them. Moreover, these factors will be likely to be changing, and there may be other factors which are not perceived at all. Wisdom in decision-making, especially within organizations, demands that these limitations be recognized. There is no 'View from Nowhere' (the title of a splendid book by Thomas Nagel). Provision needs to be made for corrigibility.

This emphasis on the value of looking at processes, and not only at 'facts of the situation', was highly congenial to me, and still more so as my mind turned more in that direction.

Barnard's book is also relevant where he speaks about the role morality of higher executives. There will be conflicts between the moral demands of the person's various roles, for instance towards the organization, his subordinates, his family. There will be tensions between personal relationships and the impersonal ones proper to a professional setting. A person will need high intelligence as well as what Barnard is prepared to call 'moral creativeness' to see possible solutions in conflicts of this kind and to know how to deal with the pressures put upon him. Where people are in positions where their abilities are insufficient and they are lacking in moral creativeness, they are apt to crack and deteriorate, especially in their power of taking responsibility.

> The moral complications of the executive functions, then, can only be endured by those possessing a commensurate ability. While, on one hand, the requisite ability without an adequate complex of moralities or without a high sense of responsibility leads to the hopeless confusion of inconsistent expediencies so often described as 'incompetence', on the other hand, the requisite morality and sense of responsibility without commensurate abilities leads to fatal indecision or emotional and impulsive decisions, with personal breakdown and ultimate destruction of the sense of responsibility. The important distinctions of rank lie in the fact that the higher the grade the more complex the *moralities* involved, and

the more necessary higher abilities to discharge the responsibilities, that is, to resolve the moral conflicts implicit in the position.[13]

Chester Barnard's book was a splendid expression of what I had been trying to say about the interplay of the three factors – personal creativity ('powers'), functions carried our through roles, and the ability to think purposively about what one is trying to do.

I had been critical of the sufficiency of Functionalism as a method in sociology and anthropology. Nowadays Anthony Giddens speaks of the demise of what had been the 'orthodox consensus of naturalistic functionalism',[14] and Jon Elster is even more caustic about presenting functional effects as explanations, and indeed even of finding good examples of feed-back loops.[15] Some contemporary sociologists are taking up Decision Theory and Games Theory[16] both of which concentrate on the factor of Purpose. There is little interest here in looking for unintended beneficial consequences. Functionalists may have looked at games through the eyes of old-fashioned public schoolmasters, as good for morals and helping young people work off their sexual urges. Games theorists will look at how a player can increase his chances of winning. Yet with all its warts, in turning attention to unintended consequences of activities within networks of institutions, Functionalism was concerned with what I think should be a central interest of sociologists and anthropologists.

While I was largely concerning myself with these, it might be thought peripheral, philosophical interests, more strictly professional ones were being promoted by Arthur Prior. He came to the Philosophy Department in Manchester in 1958, when we had authority for a second chair, and was there until he went to Oxford in 1966, dying comparatively young in 1969. His main achievement was the creation of a system of Tense Logic. I cannot speak with any knowledgeable insight about this; those interested will find it in his books *Past, Present and Future* (Oxford, Clarendon Press, 1967) and *Papers on Time and Tense* (Oxford, Clarendon Press, 1968).[17] His interests in philosophy were far wider that these highly technical ones, and he and his wife Mary made a strong personal and social contribution to the life of the Department. As a testimony to this, I repeat what I wrote in the *Guardian* after his death.

As a close colleague of Arthur Prior in the Philosophy Department of the University of Manchester, may I supplement your obituary notice by saying something about what we owed him during his time as a professor there from 1959–66? He was not only one of the most productive of contemporary philosophers, but besides taking formal classes he was also constantly in the thick of informal discussions, both technically and less technically connected with philosophy in which he had a wide sweep of interests.

He attracted research students from all over the world, and did much to build up the honours school, particularly by launching a new joint honours course in Mathematics and Philosophy. Members of the department during those year will remember with affection the parties he and his wife held in their house, with babies of married students in carry-cots in a bedroom so that wives should not be left out. He had a gift of making senior and junior members of the Department feel they were part of an extended family, and this not by setting up a consultative committee, but as a way of working and playing which came naturally to him. He was not only a good philosopher, but an unpretentiously good man.

And those were good days for the Philosophy Department.

10

Retirement with Philosophers and Friends in Cambridge: Richard Braithwaite and Margaret Masterman

I took early retirement in 1966 and, Oxford person though I was, I went to live in Cambridge. I had become close friends with Richard and Margaret Braithwaite (Masterman) and they invited me to share their house. I also had an old mother and aunt in Saffron Walden, and needed to be with them frequently; it was a short car drive from Cambridge. Personal reasons apart, I have never regretted coming to Cambridge. Oxford is now a large city with colleges in it; Cambridge is a university and market town, and that is an environment in which I like to live. More importantly, I have felt very much at home with the Cambridge philosophers. The Philosophy Faculty is not large, and its members hold a variety of views. Oxford has a great many philosophers, and, to the outsider at least, they seem to be something of a big in-group. I except the older members, now retired or shortly retiring, Dick Hare, for instance, Michael Dummett, Jonathan Cohen. In a still earlier period Gilbert Ryle always gave me a welcome in Oxford; he was also President of the Alexander Society, the Manchester students' philosophical club.

Another reason for linking up with the Braithwaites was a shared interest in thinking about religion from within the vocation of doing philosophy. Each of us had a very different philosophy, but we believed it must combine critical analysis of concepts with empirical reference where there was a question of fact. This was not a strict demand for verification, but a demand that an allegedly true factual statement should not be compatible with every possible state of affairs. We were also opposed to views which made religion immune to any empirical reference, either by making faith a matter of revelation, or of accepting theological dogma, or of allowing infinitely elastic interpretations for what might be contrary evidence, or attempts to make religion secure as a matter of purely aesthetic enjoyment of poetic symbolism. Such views put religion outside the purview of science, even of an enlarged scientific-cum-metaphysical view of what might be the nature of things. They are seductive views, not least perhaps to scientists. We resisted making religion secure in a separate frame of reference; if it had to do with truth about the nature of things, it would have to survive in the same world as science (albeit an enlarged science which would perforce have some metaphysical features).

An informal group of people, not all professionally philosophers, but sharing this kind of outlook and wanting to explore it further, came together, calling themselves the Epiphany Philosophers. The name sounds esoteric, if not presumptuous. The explanation was simply that the original members, Richard and Margaret Braithwaite and Mary Hoskyns, had been Associates of the Anglican Community of the Epiphany in Truro, where they used to visit, and they were encouraged by its then Novice Mistress, Sister Emily. I became another member of the group. Ted Bastin, a physicist, also living in the Braithwaite household, was one of its founder members.

From the beginning we discovered our closest affinities in religious circles were with members of religious orders, rather than with parochial clergy or members of the Divinity Faculty. This was because our interest was in 'contemplative' religion (in a sense about which I shall say more presently) and in its effects on ways in which people lived together; we sat loose to theology and still looser to Church politics.

Besides the Community of the Epiphany we had help from Sister Hilary of the Sisters of St Margaret who had opened a house called Neale House in Cambridge, and we had good friends in the Society of the Sacred Mission in Kelham, some of whose ablest people used to come to study philosophy in Cambridge. These supporters and friends have now nearly all died. Neale House has closed and the religious communities themselves are dwindling.

We decided to start a journal which would explore the interface of science, philosophy and religion. We called it *Theoria to Theory*, a title which was perhaps insufficiently self-explanatory, but which we thought set out what we were trying to do. This was to form a bridge between '*theoria*', the old Greek word for contemplative insight, and critical theories which could live together with scientific theories. I shall quote from the first editorial; it is hard-hitting and not very polite, but we saw no reason to be polite.

> Whitehead has a saying 'Seek simplicity and distrust it'. To our clerical friends we say: a defect in most current religious thinking has been a desire for simplicity, which will provide the easy answer to the not very penetrating question. In this journal we hope not to fall victim to the simpliste fallacy, whatever else we may fall victim to. We expect our readers to use their minds; in fact to work hard on matters to which they are not accustomed. There is no greater mistake than to think that what is true is what appeals to the masses.
>
> To our monastic friends we say: Renew your vision and when you have renewed it, display it.
>
> To our humanist friends we say: This journal is serious, and you know as well as we do that the questions it deals with are serious and cannot be laughed off. If the besetting fault of the clerical mind is superficiality, the besetting fault of the scientist is to assume that what he cannot deal with does not exist.
>
> To the philosophers we say: Stop limiting philosophy and defining it in such a way as to exclude a large number of important enquiries. Stop trying to be fashionable. Be curious! Everything else would follow if you would have some curiosity.
>
> To those who would not classify themselves with any of these, but who still hope there may be something in Christianity or indeed in any other religion, we would simply say: Things aren't as hopeless as you might think. There are more things in heaven and earth than are dreamt of in any of the philosophies currently in use. *Nil illegitime carborundum*, which is hot dog Latin for, Don't let the bastards grind you down.

In trying to promote the journal, we put a pile of copies on a book stall at a meeting of the British Council of Churches, with a notice saying WHEN YOU ARE TIRED OF TALKING ABOUT SEX, WHY NOT THINK ABOUT TRUTH? But, as we said in an editorial, 'it did no good; people are never tired of talking about sex', and this is even more so now than it was then.

The journal ran for 48 issues, spread over 15 years. It brought us a number of friends and a fair amount of controversy. We published a wide range of articles, not all directly related to the main theme, but illustrating the rich interests open to anyone prepared to be curious about the nature of things and prepared to do some philosophical thinking. We had to close down in 1981 owing to lack of resources. Renford Bambrough wrote warmly about it in *Philosophy* (January 1982) noting, as we had, the overlap in our breadth of interests and those shown then (and now) in *Philosophy*, also noting our having exempted that journal from our attack on the narrowness of much professional philosophy.

We were not, as I have said, exploring these questions through Theology, except where Theology was what the Greek Fathers of the Church called *Theologia*, speaking of spiritual matters from inspired insight; it was indeed sometimes said by these writers that there had only been three 'theologians': St John the Evangelist, St Gregory Nazianus and St Simeon the New Theologian.[1]

The word 'contemplative' has been used of this approach. It is difficult to say just what it means. It is not the same as 'mystical', which is itself a term not easily defined and covering a wide range. We were obviously sympathetic to some forms of mysticism, though I doubt if many of us could aspire to being called mystics. 'Contemplation', in the sense in which it was linked with the Greek *Theoria*, I take to be broadly a quiet receptivity, in which one is open to truth. Such 'truth' may come as an initial imprecise insight; philosophers must then move on to critical thinking. It is not 'self-authenticating'. This contemplative attitude may be what Simone Weil called 'attention'. Clearly it is not a theory, or even thinking. But it is a state of mind out of which thinking can come, and sometimes also an outgoing love – and this I find impressive. A spirit of 'attention' can be shared by scientists and philosophers as well as religiously-minded people. Ways in which it has been characterized include Plato's love of the Good, Aristotle's peak of the theoretic life, and Spinoza's *Amor Dei Intellectualis*. In all these settings 'philosophy' was connected with a way of life[2], and in the Christian setting (though not only there) this has been what Richard Braithwaite called an 'agapeistic' way of life, expressive of love.

From the beginning the Epiphany Philosophers believed that the exploration of religion should not only be an intellectual discipline, but also a discipline in learning how to live together. We could not do this in the way monastic communities can. We were of both sexes, some married with families, most with jobs, and generally scattered about the country. However, for a number of years we came together four times a year in a converted windmill on the saltings of the Norfolk coast. These gatherings were for a week of combined tough intellectual discussions, sharing the domestic chores, and holding daily 'offices', prayers with periods of quiet.

The group has now diminished. Most of the older generation have died, and the middle-aged and young ones are widely scattered with responsible jobs. But we remain in touch, and I think individuals have worked out in their own ways what they learnt through the Epiphany Philosophers. In the next chapter I shall try to say something about how I myself am coming to see some of these matters. Now, however, I come back to my main theme: the philosophers and friends among whom I was living in Cambridge.

First among them were Richard and Margaret Braithwaite. Margaret died in 1986, Richard in 1990. I shall try to say something about how I saw them.[3]

RICHARD BRAITHWAITE

There is a story that when Richard Braithwaite was visiting New York in 1968 he was invited to give a lecture to the Philosophy Society of Columbia University. But their student body was on all-out strike, and when he got there he was met by a picket who told him they had closed the University. Richard said he was due to speak to the Philosophy Society. The picket said there would be no meeting, and he was sorry as he was a student of philosophy himself, whereupon Richard proceeded to give his talk to the picket and receive his comments.

The story illustrates Richard's zest for philosophy and his readiness to engage in discussion with anyone who was serious about it. Frivolous or ill-considered remarks in philosophy, or indeed about anything else, could be met by a roar, alarming to those not used to it, but quickly subsiding. It was this combination of serious-ness with zest, relentlessly acute criticism with personal support, which made him a notable teacher. He made vigorous contributions in conferences and meetings such as those of the Moral Sciences Club, sometimes rising up and making them when he had appeared to be asleep.

Richard came up to King's in 1919 with a scholarship in Natural Science and read both parts of the Mathematical Tripos and Part II of the Moral Sciences Tripos. Keynes had spotted his ability as an undergraduate. When they first met they talked for two hours about Freud and two about *Principia Mathematica*. Keynes got him into the Political Economy Club which met weekly in his rooms. Richard might have turned to economics, but Keynes urged him to do philosophy, which, he said, was more difficult.

Whether or not this is generally true of the two subjects, it was probably true of the kind of philosophy which Richard was to pursue, in particular a mathematical philosophy of science and the Theory of Probability. He shared these interests with the brilliant mathematical philosopher-cum-economist Frank Ramsey, also a Fellow of King's. After Ramsey's tragically early death in 1930 Richard edited a collection of his papers under the title *The Foundations of Mathematics* (London, Routledge, 1931). He was glad to see the recognition which Frank Ramsey's work is winning among present-day Cambridge philosophers, and he supported Professor Hugh Mellor's bringing out a new and enlarged edition of *The Foundations of Mathematics* (London, Routledge, 1978).

He won an international reputation with his book *Scientific Explanation* (Cambridge, 1953). It shows him standing within the tradition of Empiricism but enriching it with an extension of the Hypothetico-Deductive view of Science. This included treatments of the distinction between theories and laws of nature and of the use of models; a view of probability which drew on his up-to-date knowledge of statistical methods; a pragmatic justification of induction; and a view of teleological explanation as applied to goal-directed systems. These are among the features of his work which still excite discussion.

So Braithwaite was essentially a mathematically-minded philosopher of science, but he was also, as he said of himself, an incorrigible moralist. He was not sympathetic to the kind of ethics represented by most moral philosophers, based on analyses of concepts such as 'duty', 'obligation', 'good'. In his inaugural lecture as Knightbridge Professor of Moral Philosophy, *Theory of Games as a Tool for the Moral Philosopher* (Cambridge, 1955), Decision Theory is applied to give practical advice to two bachelors, Luke and Matthew, occupying adjacent flats. Luke likes to play classical music on his piano in the evenings, and Matthew likes to improvise jazz on his trumpet. Given four possible outcomes, Luke playing and Matthew silent, Matthew playing and Luke silent, both playing and neither playing, and the order of their respective sets of preferences, Braithwaite will advise them on what distribution will combine the highest assignment to one consonant with a like highest assignment to the other and which would thus be a fair distribution. The result, reached with some beautiful indifference curves and parabolas, is that Luke should play classical music for 17 evenings to Matthew's jazz trumpeting for 26.

What we have here is an ideal case: a situation with full information limited to two persons, with no other parties such as a landlady or neighbours coming in and expressing preferences. It might be said that actual situations are seldom so circumscribed. But what Braithwaite was showing, and I think this was new at the time, was not only that Decision Theory might be of assistance in morals, but that moral considerations could come into Decision Theory: in some conflicts of interests if both parties were prepared to co-operate in a fair agreement each would do better for himself. I think it is this feature, the value of co-operation and trust, which makes a bridge to the other side of Richard's moral philosophy – the interest in people's springs of action and sincerity and insincerity as shown in actions. Here he said he got more from reading novels than from books on moral philosophy. He thought Iris Murdoch was one of the most serious moralists of our time, and he was reading and re-reading her novels up to his death, and we used to discuss them together.

Since then I have formed a philosophical friendship with Iris Murdoch over her view of 'the sovereignty of Good'. In *The Role of the Unrealisable* I suggested that the idea of the Good, as distinct from things being good for a purpose or good after their kind, could be seen as a Regulative Ideal, not definable but setting a direction for the reason. But 'Good' *simpliciter* is so far from being specifiable that it is hard to see how it gives this direction. So I find that chapter of the book far from satisfactory. Nevertheless, I still want to see the idea of the Good as a Regulative Ideal, making reference to a standard when we speak of something as good, or better than something else, or better than it was before. This gives Good a transcendental status. We approach it not directly, but through coming to appreciate the goodness of particular people and particular things. The capacity for this comes by winning freedom of spirit from what Iris Murdoch calls 'the greedy self'. Her novels show subtle ways in which this happens or fails to happen.

This leads me to try to say something about Richard's religious philosophy. He had been brought up a Quaker and was at the Quaker School, Bootham. In the First World War he said that his agonizing as a 17-year-old over whether he should be a pacifist led to his profound interest in politics and in political philosophy. He finally decided for pacifism and joined the Friend's Ambulance Unit. His greatest school friend decided the other way and was killed. Richard was uneasy as to whether his own decision had been partly motivated by the desire for self-preservation (note the interest in sincerity and springs of action). Later in life he gave up pacifism on political and intellectual grounds.

Also later in life he joined the Church of England and was baptized in King's College Chapel. This had nothing to do with the pacifist issue, but it had a lot to do with the importance he attached to co-operation. He held that if possible one should join in the form of religious observance which came nearest to helping one to co-operate with the people with whom one lived and worked, in his case his wife and family, the Epiphany Philosophers, and his College and its Chapel.

He gave his religious philosophy in the Eddington Lecture of 1955: 'An Empiricist's View of the Nature of Religious Belief' (Cambridge, 1955). A key word here is 'Belief' on which he had already formed a view. This made it partly a matter of entertaining propositions, and also, and most importantly, a matter of being prepared to act according to certain intentions. Since, as an empiricist, he held that religion contained no objectively meaningful propositions to be entertained,[4] religious belief should be seen as the intentional direction of springs of action, and its sincerity shown in how in fact one acted. The intention could be supported by the attractive power of religious stories. He counted himself a Christian because he committed himself to acting 'agapeistically' (in a spirit of love) and saw this as supported by Christian stories, especially those in the Gospels. Towards the end of the Second World War he had had a strong conversion experience which led him to see that he must re-orient his springs of action. I think he was naturally a rather self-indulgent man, and he could fall back into being this (which of us does not?) but he knew he had to bring himself back to his commitment. Religion was emphatically not a matter of feeling, but of *will*. Also, while naturally an ebullient person, he had the capacity, perhaps from his Quaker background, to put himself into a state of deep recollected quiet.

Richard took a keen interest in public affairs and in the affairs of his College and University. In university politics he said that what gave him greatest satisfaction was having, along with K.P. Harrison, prepared a memorial and collected signatures to place before the Regent House prior to the Grace admitting women to membership of the University and so also to degrees. His first wife, Dorothea Morison, who died in 1936, and his second wife Margaret Masterman, who died in 1986, were both members of Newnham College and his daughter Catherine was at Girton (his son Lewis is a Kingsman). But his concern for the cause of academic women was a matter of principle, not of family pressure. He also gave active support to Lucy Cavendish College of which Margaret was a Founding Fellow.

He had a deep love for his College. For years he had enjoyed coming into dinner, not only for the food, though his pleasure in that was not negligible, but for the intellectual conversation. He especially enjoyed talking to the younger scientific Fellows about their work and he had an unbounded curiosity about what was going on in the sciences. His election as a corresponding member of the American Academy of the Arts and Sciences gave him great pleasure. In the last few months of his life he took up the mathematics of Chaos Theory, and got information about the literature from his friend and former pupil Stephan Körner.

Indeed, he considered curiosity was a primary human virtue. Shortly before his death he said to me 'We intellectuals are very fortunate. We need never be bored.' On one occasion when he was in Addenbrooke's he was taken for an X-ray examination, and was brought back to the ward in some confusion. Then he rallied and said 'Dorothy, it was pure animal behaviourism. They didn't ask me anything; they didn't explain anything to me. They were only looking for signals from me. Pure animal behaviourism.' An apt comment. Under his physical condition, the philosopher was in working order.

MARGARET MASTERMAN

Richard's wife Margaret (Margaret Masterman) was a close friend of mine. She is difficult to categorize: she would categorize herself at various times as a philosopher, linguistic expert, novelist, religious contemplative. Sometimes these *personae* thwarted each other, at others they supported each other. The thwarting came especially when she tried to write; sentences were convoluted, several themes chased each other, and several ideas came up at once. Yet they were *ideas*. She had imaginative, unusual insights which she would throw into a discussion. Her difficulty was in working them out, supporting them by arguments, replying to criticisms. It had to fall to others to do that (if indeed it could be done), and so too in cases of practical implementation, if that was what was called for.

This was notably so with Lucy Cavendish College. Margaret had had the thought of forming a group round the blind historian, Kathleen Wood-Legh, who was doing distinguished research and a good deal of supervision, but had no college position. This group turned into a dining club of able women who were in a like situation, as indeed was Margaret. One of them was the zoologist, Anna Bidder. Margaret said to her 'you know we could form the high table of a new women's college'. They set about planning this; it involved talking to the Vice-Chancellor of the day and other leading members of the University. One of their assets consisted in Anna's late father, Sir George Bidder (also a zoologist) having laid down a cellar and word got around 'If you go and talk to these people you will get a glass of the Bidder port.' Thus do institutions get started.

Lucy Cavendish's distinctive role was to be a college for women who had been prevented through having children, looking after parents, or by other commitments, from going to the University at the usual age, or who had started research and had to drop it. In later life they might find they had the inclination to take up university work if given the opportunity. Nowadays there are a number of mature students at universities and colleges. At that time (in the early 1960s), Lucy Cavendish was a pioneering institution designed to meet their special needs. The name came from the widow of Lord Frederick Cavendish, whom Gladstone had sent to Dublin as Chief Secretary and who was murdered almost immediately in Phoenix Park. When Gladstone went to see Lucy Cavendish the first thing she said, knowing that he too was in grief, was 'Uncle William, you were quite right to send him.' She was a woman of ability who was never sent to a university; she was intensely interested in girls' education and founded the Girls' Public Day School Trust. Since male Cavendishs were commemorated by the Cavendish Laboratory, it was thought fitting that a new women's college should commemorate a remarkable female Cavendish (Margaret was her great-niece). On coming to Cambridge I was made a fellow, to my great gain as, besides giving me a college connection, I became an incorporated member of the University.

Another institution which Margaret launched was the Cambridge Language Research Unit. She had a strong concern for the philosophy of language, but not in the sense given it by Oxford philosophers like Gilbert Ryle and J.L. Austin, nor in the sense of Wittgenstein's 'language-games' (though she had been in Wittgenstein's classes in the 1930s). She wanted to discover underlying structures common across a number of different languages. These would not be the subject-predicate grammatical form. Her idea was that a piece of language should be analysed into segments, each carrying a central emphasis point. She called these segments 'breath groups', the notion being that in the spoken word, for instance when someone was making a speech, each of these segments would normally be as long as would be needed for the speaker to draw breath, and that human physiology being constant, this would be much the same in all languages. Other words were ranked in stress relation to the words of the emphasis point. Thus, this _sentence_ is an *instance* of a *breath-group*, where the emphasis point may be 'sentence'.

Margaret hoped that this kind of analysis would yield structures which could be matched in different languages, thereby aiding translation since to uncover the emphasis could show what a sentence was about. She also thought that values could be assigned to degrees of stress and emphasis, and the whole structure formalized and put on a computer. She herself was not successful in this; since her death those working at the Cambridge Language Research Unit have been producing formalizations which can be programmed, using segments called 'cognitive linguistic units'. This work has a precision which Margaret could never have achieved. But the original launch was given by Margaret's idea of the 'breath-group'.

A third area of concern – perhaps her deepest – was religion. She believed passionately in a mystical reaching out which was not a mere aberration, but a creative drive in human nature. This not only pressed forward, but, she believed, ran back into the process of biological growth, and it should be studied and interpreted through an enlarged scientific view of development. This would also be a metaphysical view, one that was teleological and non-materialistic, and she believed that the mystical drive was an expression of a universal principle; she called it the Logos. Again, ideas were launched imaginatively, but the book in which they might have been worked out was never written. She did, however, produce occasional pieces, some given as lectures. Rowan Williams (now Bishop of Monmouth) and I collected some of them and they were privately produced under the title 'Religious Explorations'. They are not easy reading; nothing that Margaret wrote ever was. Those who knew Margaret may, however, be able to hear her speaking through them.[5]

Some of Margaret's ideas about contemplative religion were like those to which I drew attention in writing about the Epiphany Philosophers. Indeed, the initial ideas behind this group came mainly from Margaret, as did those behind the journal *Theoria to Theory*. Margaret's father, C.F.G. Masterman (a Cabinet Minister in Asquith's Liberal Government) and her mother, Lucy Masterman, went in for the higher journalism as well as being politicians, and Margaret herself had acquired some of the necessary skills, including the capacity to make a wide range of contacts. Others could do the actual production.

To return to her own religious philosophy. Towards the end she believed that the deepest and characteristically Christian activity was what she called 'passionistic'. It included self-sacrificial action, but it could also be found in extreme circumstances, as under sentence of death or in great physical suffering. The supreme note was *joy*; this was not masochistic pleasure, but an inner ecstatic experience. Christ's death was the archetypal exemplar of passionistic activity; though she questioned whether Jesus himself in his Passion achieved this joy. Yet does her claim that there should be joy *in extremis* go so far as to be a dramatic idealization? Not to have joy at such times may not be a mark of spiritual failure: sometimes willingness to accept and go through the suffering may be a positive affirmation; and perhaps it will be found that 'joy cometh in the morning'. I do not know; Margaret was strongly resistant to anything she saw as a watering down. Her enemies were convention and stereotypy. As Rowan Williams said at her memorial service, 'Margaret's Christianity was visionary, turbulent and idiosyncratic; but in conclusion it must be said that it rested on a fundamentally simple conviction that change and forgiveness and newness are possible. She understood a great deal herself about offering and needing forgiveness, and that part of her witness will always remain a clear and sobering memory for her friends.' I endorse this.

Margaret died in 1986 distressingly of motor neurone disease. Richard died rather suddenly in 1990. Since then I have come even closer to Cambridge philosophers. They may not agree with my views – why should they? – and they hold differing views themselves. Along with members of my family they produced a splendid party for my ninetieth birthday. This was mainly organized by Professor Hugh Mellor and Dr Onora O'Neill, Principal of

1. Dorothy Emmet and Bryan Magee at her 90th birthday party, with acknowledgement to D. H. Mellor.

2. A. D. Lindsay. With acknowledgement to Drusilla Scott.

3. Alfred North Whitehead. Photograph taken for the tercentenary of Harvard
    University 1936. This appeared in the British Academy obituary memoir of
    A. N. Whitehead by Dorothy Emmet (*Proceedings*, Vol. xxxiii) and is
    reproduced by permission.

4. Samuel Alexander. Photograph by F. W. Schmidt, with acknowledgement to the University of Manchester.

11

Retrospect and Prospect

I am generally averse to looking back at past writings. Life moves on, and one hopes that one's thinking also moves on. Here, however, I have been looking back in the company of philosophers and friends, and recalling what they have given me. At certain points I have said that I would come back to how certain interests I mentioned look to me now, and I must therefore try to say something, however summarily, about them.

Two have been in the background, a political interest and a religious interest. Clearly interests should not shape conclusions, but it is right and proper to bring them into one's philosophy. So first, the political interest. Here in principle I stand by the view of moral democracy I got from Lindsay. But it is more difficult to sustain this now. We are more aware of the intractability of the economic substructure – for instance, *pace* Keynes, unemployment and inflation can come together and measures to curb the one can exacerbate the other. This sort of problem preoccupies us now, rather than the debate with the Marxists. Then there is the question of Sovereignty. In principle I think Lindsay was right: Sovereignty is not a matter of political power but of constitutional rules pre-scribing where final powers of decision lie. Our problem is how far these should rest with the unitary nation state or how far powers of decision-making for different purposes should be distributed and to whom. The old tag, that 'Sovereignty can be neither limited nor divided' is no longer applicable.

Moreover, Lindsay's view of democracy was over-sanguine about the beneficial large-scale effects of the activities of small-scale voluntary organizations. He was surely right to give them a role in a democratic civic culture, but this role is more circumscribed by the nature of the economy than he allowed; it is also more difficult to carry it out now that the partnership of mutual support (including financial support) between statutory and voluntary bodies has been weakened.

I think Lindsay was right in saying that some infusion of the morality of 'grace' needs to come even into the world of political power struggles. I myself, writing about this[1], have called it the 'x factor', and described it as 'generosity of spirit'. Is this in increasingly short supply in contemporary politics? If we compare Lindsay's views with those of Reinhold Niebuhr, who also tried to develop a Christian democratic political philosophy, we find that Niebuhr is more conscious of the temptations of even idealistic groups to see the public interest in the perspective of their own interests. Like Lindsay, he saw political life in the context of an ultimate transcendent ideal, and, like Lindsay, he interprets it in terms of the Gospel teaching about perfection. But he saw this as an 'impossible possibility' whose function is to keep us humbly free from any complacency about the achievements, compromises, accommodations, in our social behaviour. It is therefore a remote vision, cleansing and chastening, rather than, as was Lindsay's, an 'operative ideal' which can bring something of the generosity and compassion of the morality of grace into this social behaviour. Here Lindsay probably has a truer understanding of how numbers of politically devoted people in all walks of democratic politics actually live and work. But Niebuhr is probably more realistic about the abrasive, intractable problems of power politics and economics in large impersonal societies, especially on an international scale.

I was aware of a strong influence from Niebuhr in writing my recent book, *The Role of the Unrealisable*. It is a very anti-Utopian book, but also, I hope, a study in the right as well as the wrong use of absolutes in political as well as personal morality. I found help in the Kantian notion of the Regulative Ideal, never fully achievable, but setting an orientation for practical reason and showing a direction in which to go. To keep one's sights on a Regulative Ideal enables one to avoid Utopianism and moralism without falling into cynicism.

Then there was the religious interest. I have said that I came to see that there was a choice between philosophy and religion, or rather theology. I must explain how I make the distinction with theology. In 1950 I gave the Stanton Lectures in the Philosophy of Religion in Cambridge and daringly gave them the title 'Religious Language'. The lectures were abortive and I never published them. But I still hold to a distinction I was trying to make between what I called three 'orders' of religious language. The first was highly concrete, generally personalized and a language of faith and devotion, for example 'The Lord is my Shepherd, therefore can I lack nothing.' The second is the theological language, which constructs doctrines, as a systematic presentation of the teachings of some religious tradition. Theological 'second order' language draws on forms of thought from some available type of philosophy, for instance the Platonic or Aristotelian, and it also draws on the symbols of a religious tradition which it seeks to express theoretically. So we might have 'the Doctrine of Providence', and 'the Doctrine of Creation' where a philosophical notion of First Cause merges with a religious notion of personal will. Then there is the 'third order' language of philosophy, which tries to probe more analytically into the theological as well as the primary religious language, to say something critically about what these expressions might mean. So doctrines of creation will be examined by taking a hard look at the notion of Causation. Natural Theology can come close to being a form of philosophy insofar as it is an attempt to think in a general way about these questions without being beholden to some particular tradition. It is probably not possible to attain complete detached generality – the natural theologians of the eighteenth century, for instance, were quite prepared to talk about 'the Author of Nature'. Nor are philosophers as detached as all that; we do not have what Hilary Putnam calls a 'God's eye view' and Thomas Nagel 'the view from nowhere'. It is perhaps a matter of how far one will go on probing while remembering that probing need not be the same as deconstruction; there is the possibility and the hope that there will be something positive which can be said. But it is not at all easy to say what it is philosophically; this may be why the *Theoria to Theory* enterprise did not get further.

Here I quote from a letter written to me years ago by an older friend, F.A. Cockin (later to be Bishop of Bristol). I found it inside my copy of Collingwood's *Speculum Mentis*. 'George' Cockin (as we called him) had been an undergraduate friend of Collingwood's at Oxford, he and I had both been reading that controversial book. He writes

> I haven't recovered from *Speculum Mentis* yet, even though I know that it is scorned and spat upon by Oxford generally. I do think – the evidence seems to me more and more to support it – that religion is something quite distinct and different from science and philosophy. Well, God and immortality (or Resurrection rather) and prayer and all these things are the business – the stock in trade – of religion – and jolly good stuff too – and only a fool turns up his nose at it and thinks he can 'expose' or 'explain' or 'dispense'

with it. And religion gives you *truth* – but truth wrapped up in its own particular words and forms which it itself can never distinguish and separate from the truth which they enshrine. This is the business of philosophy which takes the cherished beliefs of religion one by one and examines them. 'What do you mean by God?' is essentially a philosophical not a religious question, and once that has begun you have got out of the specifically religious stage which says 'I believe in God' into the philosophical which says '"God" means ...'

A dualism you think. No, but an infinitely difficult and as Von Hügel would say *costing* choice. And when you have made your choice you find that amid all the wreckage of the old stuff there is a small collection of new truth which looks astonishingly unlike the old but on further examination turns out to be the genuine article which the old really contained though it didn't know it, couldn't say it and would have burnt you at the stake for saying this was really the same as this new stuff of yours.

I gave my own estimate of *Speculum Mentis* when I was discussing Collingwood in Chapter 2, and I said that I thought that he distinguished the different forms of thought too sharply, setting them in stages, and also I had reservations about philosophy as an absolute form of thought. I think too that the boundaries between my three 'orders' of religious language are not always sharp. There are many varieties of religion and so too of theology, and some may look like forms of philosophy, or quasi-philosophy, from the start, and some not at all. So Buddhism, as Whitehead said, is 'a metaphysic generating a religion', whereas Christianity 'has always been' (and still is?) 'a religion seeking a metaphysic'.[2] But this distinction, still more the Collingwood-Cockin distinction, of the different stages, and my own of the three orders of language, are in effect 'ideal types' rather than instances as found in practice. Here some philosophy can get into a religion, and some religion into a philosophy, and theology has elements of both. Buddhist metaphysics, with its doctrine of karma and its search for enlightenment, is not only a pure philosophy. And Spinoza's great climax in the *Amor Dei Intellectualis* is surely a religious vision from within philosophy – perhaps the greatest there has ever been. Nevertheless ideal types are of value in highlighting distinctions which help us to see real differences in aim and emphasis where choices must be made. I think George Cockin's insistence on there being a real and costing choice stands. He may be going too far in saying that you may come to some 'new stuff' in philosophy which you will be able to see is what the old religious stuff was really about. But it may be possible to think that it represents some aspect of 'the old stuff'; you may see why people should have wanted to use first order religious language about it, and you may even find it possible to use some of it yourself.

Then have I any philosophical stuff which I see in this way? Primarily it is connected with a belief that we live in what I would like to call an 'enabling universe'. This sounds rather like what is called the Anthropic Principle, and so perhaps it is, but in my own sense. There is a strong and a weak sense of the Anthropic Principle. The strong sense is highly teleological; it claims that since the universe has produced such remarkable beings as ourselves, it was designed to do so. But the universe has also produced a vast range of other kinds of beings, and the ways it has done so, and the kinds of adjustments and lack of adjustments between them, do not look like products at any rate of any kind of personal design. There is also the scale of the universe – the large scale of billions of light years and the small scale of sub-atomic particles – and all this seems highly counter-intuitive if thought about in terms of human-centred design. Also, arguments from or to Design use concepts of ordinary language. But the world as it is coming to seem in the new physics seems totally unlike the world as described in ordinary language. So I cannot take the Anthropic Principle in its strong form. In its weak form it is in effect the modal argument from actuality to possibility: since we are actually here, it must be possible for us to be here. I do not find that the Anthropic Principle in its weak form therefore says anything impressive.

Nevertheless, my view might be considered to be a strengthening of the weak form of the Anthropic Principle. It is not only that because we are actually here, it must be possible for us to be here, but that the universe contains resources which have made it possible. This is why I have used the expression 'an enabling universe'.

'Enabling' is an activity word. It means doing things that produce conditions or support, or both, which make it possible for other things to be done. We speak politically of the 'Enabling State', meaning the kind of Welfare State which does not normally directly do things for people, but provides them with conditions and support so that they are able to do them. Could the Universe be thought of as a vast Enabling State? In a way, I think yes, provided we also see it as having features of a free market of a fairly ruthlessly competitive kind, in which the weakest may go to the wall. This is called Natural Selection; the term is used chiefly, though not exclusively, of how organisms succeed or fail to find niches in which the supporting factors are sufficient for them to be able to survive, grow, perpetuate their kind. So Natural Selection presupposes a world in which there are possibilities of interactive support. There are also the probing activities whereby organisms seek out a niche and have the capacity not only to adapt to one but sometimes also to modify it. All this looks like more than just jostling for position; it makes the world look like a theatre in which mutual support can get established.

I am only sketching out how I see this vast and controversial subject. The biologist whom I find most sympathetic in these matters is C.H. Waddington.[3] I called attention to how he acknowledged an influence from Whitehead, in seeing an organism as a 'concrescence of prehensions', a process of self-formation through active responses to elements in its environment.

I emphasize *active*. If we go below the biological to the physical world, the picture is one of interrelated patterns of energy. 'Energy' has its technical meaning as a measure of work. But 'work' is an activity word, something effected; there is energetic activity. In its original Greek meaning *energeia* is actuality as distinct from potentiality (*dynamis*). I find it significant that *energeia* in Greek is an activity word – it is not the modern notion of a measure of work, but of existence or being as an active state capable therefore of work. This I find congenial. I have long distinguished between a strong sense of existence, where *esse est operari*, from the weak sense, where, as Quine puts it, 'to be is to be the value of a variable'. The latter has a use wherever there can be existential quantification over some description. Existential quantification enables us to say that prime numbers, as well as cabbages and kings, exist, and that there are some things like unicorns that don't exist. Many philosophers say that this is all we need for 'exists'. But I have never felt that it was all I needed. I accept the weak sense of logical existential quantification, but I also want metaphysically to have a strong sense in which to exist is to have a capacity to act and to make a difference to other things.

I realize thinking back that in nearly everything I have written I have been interested in kinds of activities. I have been mindful (though perhaps not explicitly as such) of what Whitehead called 'The Fallacy of Misplaced Concreteness'. I have not wanted a world which would be, in Bradley's words, 'a spectral woof of impalpable abstractions', nor one in which abstract nouns could govern active verbs, that is be represented as doing things (even as in common expressions, for example 'Science teaches us to look for evidence', where what is meant is that if we are doing science we learn that we should look for evidence). There is an underlying actual activity, and it is well to recognize this.

So I have looked at forms of activity, how they differ and how they support or frustrate each other. This was particularly so in *Function, Purpose and Powers*, where I was considering societies as needing to contain networks of institutions where interrelated activities could be mutually supportive without having been planned as such – the then currently fashionable 'functional' model. There were also the purposive activities in which some people individually or co-operatively try to instil some direction into some of what is going on. And there were the activities coming from what with some hesitation I called 'powers', the capacity of some people, not all of them by any means ones who might be called 'great', to bring in some novelty of approach, ideas, ways of behaving. I claimed that a society needs an infusion of creative activity for its vitality if not for its survival. In my *Rules, Roles and Relations*, I was coming closer to showing how streamlined social activities worked through roles carried out with a measure of individual discretion and initiative; where this is lacking we get stereotypy if not deadlock.

On the human scene we have networks of interrelated activities going on with more and with less success, the success depending on supporting circumstances and also on interjections of individual creativity. When I tried to write about morality (as in *The Moral Prism*) I looked beyond the moral concepts of principles and ends to the nature of moral judgement in problematic situations and the ways in which it can be fostered. At one time I did a certain amount of work on Coleridge as a philosopher, following a piece 'Coleridge on the Growth of the Mind'[4] which aroused a certain amount of interest among literary critics and was anthologized several times.[5] I went into his self-knowledge of the inner conditions for the active powers of his 'shaping spirit of imagination', when they worked and when, as all too often, they failed to work. Among the latter conditions he listed not only the habits of the 'lazy indolent', but also those of the 'busy indolent' who find ways of occupying their energies without ever having seriously to rouse themselves to think. In writing about events and processes (in *The Passage of Nature* and elsewhere) I have claimed that neither an event nor a process ontology is sustainable on its own; if there are to be *actions*, neither events nor processes can act, and they need to have participants who can.

So I see the world as a theatre of activities, in which participants enter processes, some mutually supportive, some mutually destructive. Things in process form, dissolve, re-form, and sometimes produce a new kind with capabilities for new kinds of activity. So I have been interested in possibilities of creative processes and their conditions, and I think that some of my former religious interest has gone into this. Of course, creativity and the conditions for creativity, for instance in the arts and sciences, need not be ostensibly religious. Nor need religion necessarily be a force for creativity, any more than it need necessarily be good. It can make for stereotypy and for repression and violence, as notably in the rising power of fundamentalism, Christian as well as Islamic, and also in some of the sects. It gives strong motivation and capacity for sacrifice, and this can be in defence or proclamation of a doctrine or in commitment to a cause.

Yet there can be and is religious creativity, strengthening, renewing, shown in freedom of spirit and in a capacity for outgoing love. Love, we know, can be possessive and jealous. Where it is free from these qualities, and where it reaches out in a wider generosity, it seems to come from a deep root of the psyche beyond particular emotions and beyond the level of consciousness. Yet unlike the more superficial unconscious urges it is not turbulent and self-gratifying. This strength, coming from what the old mystics called the 'fundus' of the soul, is where, religiously speaking, I look for creative power. It may be an expression in human life of a wider creative power and we may see it as divine power – or this may be an 'over-belief'. At any rate, the power comes as of 'grace', and some religious language becomes meaningful in living from this root. This is, perhaps, particularly so over forgiveness, reconciliation, renewal of relationships, and in finding a constructive outcome where a situation has gone wrong. The enabling universe in its creative energy contains resources for such possibilities. These do not only come alive in religious contexts, though nonetheless they may be religiously impressive. They may be part of what in religious language is called grace. I ended my *The Role of the Unrealisable* by referring to Reinhold Niebuhr's use of the text 'We are perplexed but not in despair.' I pointed out that St Paul's actual words contain a cadence and metaphor which this translation misses – *aporourmenoi all' ouk exaporourmenoi* – 'we cannot find the way but we are not utterly at a dead end'.[6]

I should like to think that this is so in doing philosophy.

Notes

CHAPTER 2
PHILOSOPHY IN OXFORD IN THE 1920s:
H.A. PRICHARD AND R.G. COLLINGWOOD

1. I criticized this Idealist view, but in relation to Bradley and not to Joachim, in my British Academy Lecture (1949) 'Presuppositions and Finite Truths' (Proceedings of the British Academy Vol. 35) and in the chapter 'True Propositions and Truth as a Regulative Ideal' in my book *The Role of the Unrealisable* (London, 1994).
2. R.G. Collingwood, *Autobiography* (Oxford: Clarendon Press, 1939) p. 119.

CHAPTER 3
A.D. LINDSAY: PHILOSOPHY AND MORAL DEMOCRACY

1. Something of this ambiguity comes up over the use of the term 'representations' by the cognitive psychologists.
2. A.D. Lindsay, 'Philosophy as a Criticism of Standards', *Philosophical Quarterly*, vol. 1 (1950) no. 2. It was also reprinted in the collection of *Selected Addresses*, 1957 (privately published).
3. I have considered some of these distinctions while generalizing the notion of Regulative Ideals in my *The Role of the Unrealisable* (London, 1994).
4. *The Two Moralities* (London, Eyre and Spottiswode, 1940), p. 41.
5. *Proceedings of the Aristotelian Society*, Supplementary Volume VIII, (1928), 'Bosanquet's Theory of the General Will'.
6. *Proceedings of the Aristotelian Society* 1923–1924.
7. As Professor A.B. Ulam did in his *Philosophical Foundations of English Socialism* (Harvard, 1951), which contains a brief and appreciative though critical account of Lindsay's views, especially in Chapter VIII, 'The State and Neo-Idealism'.

    [In this chapter I have drawn on the chapter 'Lindsay as Philosopher' which I contributed to *A.D. Lindsay: a Biography* by Drusilla Scott (1974). I am grateful to Drusilla Scott and the publishers, Basil Blackwell, for permission to do this.]

CHAPTER 5
A.N. WHITEHEAD IN CAMBRIDGE, MASS.

1. V. Lowe, *Understanding Whitehead*, p. 276 (Johns Hopkins 1962).
2. I have gone into this at some length in my paper 'Whitehead's view of Causal Efficacy' in the Proceedings of the Bonn Symposium, *Whitehead und der Prozessbegriff* (Alber Verlag, 1984).

3. 'The Practical Consequences of Metaphysical Beliefs on a Biologist's Work' in C.H. Waddington, *Towards a Theoretical Biology* 2, p. 76 (Edinburgh 1969).
4. A.N. Whitehead, *Process and Reality*, p. 19 (all references are to the Corrected Edition, New York and London, Free Press, 1978).
5. A.N. Whitehead, *Modes of Thought* (Cambridge, 1938) p. 232.
6. In *A.N. Whitehead: Essays on his Philosophy*: ed. G.L. Kline (Englewood Cliffs, 1963).
7. *Process and Reality*, p. 40.
8. *Process and Reality*, Part I, chapter ii, section 2.
9. I refer anyone interested in what I have tried to say further about them to my papers 'Whitehead's view of Causal Efficacy' in *Whitehead und du Prozessbegriff* and 'Creativity and the Passage of Nature' in *Whitehead's Metaphysik der Kreativität* (Alber Verlag 1986): translated by F. Rapp and R. Wiehl, *Whitehead's Metaphysics of Creativity* (State University of New York Press, 1990).

CHAPTER 6
POLITICS AND PHILOSOPHY IN THE 1930s: JOHN MACMURRAY AND REINHOLD NIEBUHR

1. *Recollections of Wittgenstein*, edited by Rush Rhees, p. 123 (Oxford University Press, 1984).
2. D. Emmet, *The Role of the Unrealisable; a Study in Regulative Ideals* (1994).
3. See above, Chapter 3, pp. 22–4.
4. R. Niebuhr, *An Interpretation of Christian Ethics*, pp. 60–1 (Harpers, New York and London, 1935).

CHAPTER 7
SAMUEL ALEXANDER IN MANCHESTER

1. *Philosophical and Literary Pieces*, ed. J. Laird, p. 27 (London, Macmillan, 1939).
2. From the Memoir by J. Laird, *Philosophical and Literary Pieces*, pp. 72–3.
3. S. Alexander, *Space, Time and Deity* I, p. 4 (London, Macmillan, 1920).
4. *Space, Time and Deity* I, p. 58.
5. R.G. Collingwood, *An Essay on Metaphysics* (Oxford, Clarendon Press, 1940) ch. vii, especially pp. 176–7.
6. See above, p. 14.
7. My source of this information is Brian McGuinness' *Wittgenstein: a Life* (London, Duckworth, 1988) p. 75. McGuinness obtained it from R.L. Goodstein's account, given on pp. 171 and 172 in Ambrose and Lazwrowitz, *Ludwig Wittgenstein, Philosopher of Language* (1972). So it comes at several hands.
8. Drury's recollection was given to McGuiness in a personal communication (referred to by McGuiness, op. cit., p. 75).

CHAPTER 8
PHILOSOPHY IN MANCHESTER: RELIGION AND METAPHYSICS. MICHAEL POLANYI

1. C.C.J. Webb, *Religion and Theism* (London, 1934).
2. W. Temple, *Nature, Man and God*, p. 56 (London, Macmillan 1934).
3. For these, see 'Logic and Reality', *Aristotelian Society Supplementary Volume* XX (1946).
4. J. Polanyi, *The Logic of Personal Knowledge. Essays presented to Michael Polanyi on his Seventieth Birthday* (London, Routledge, 1961).
5. J.L. Austin, *How to do things with Words*, Lecture IX (Oxford, Clarendon Press, 1962).
6. Op. cit., Chapter 7. True propositions and Truth as a Regulative Ideal.
7. I owe this distinction between the big T and the little t's to William James, though his use of it is rather different.

CHAPTER 9
PHILOSOPHY IN MANCHESTER: THEORIES IN THE SOCIAL SCIENCES . ALASDAIR MACINTYRE AND MAX GLUCKMAN

1. *Sociological Theory and Philosophical Analysis*, (London, Macmillan, 1970). Papermac Edition in Macmillan Student Editions.
2. Kobundo publishers, 1976.
3. A MacIntyre (1980), *After Virtue*, p. 263.
4. This is not incompatible with what I said about Hart's criticism of the conceptual confusions in how philosophers have treated topics like 'rights'. For Hart a legal system has a rule of recognition for what is or is not a rule of the system, and thus it is less conflated with a moral system.
5. D. Emmet, *Function, Purpose and Powers* (London, Macmillan, 1958; 2nd edn 1972).
6. A. Radcliffe Brown, *Structure and Function of a Primitive Society* (London, 1952) p. 180.
7. R. Merton, *Social Theory and Social Structure* (Illinois Free Press, 1951).
8. Richard Stone, *Some British Empiricists in the Social Sciences*. Cambridge University Press, forthcoming.
9. I am not of course referring to 'powers' in the sense of a legally or constitutionally defined ability to do something.
10. The whole description can be read in Sartre's *L'Etre et le Néant*. English translation by Hazel E. Barnes, *Being and Nothingness* (London, Methuen, 1957) p. 59.
11. Sir Geoffrey Vickers, *The Art of Judgement*, pp. 60–1 (London 1965).
12. C. Barnard, *The Functions of the Executive* (Harvard 1938). Whiteheadian influence is acknowledged on p. 195.
13. *The Functions of the Executive*, p. 276.
14. A. Giddens, *Social Theory and Modern Sociology* (Oxford, Blackwell, 1987) p. 24.

15. J. Elster, *Ulysses and the Sirens* (Cambridge, 1979) pp. 28 ff.
16. See the papers in *Rational Choice*, ed. Jon Elster (Oxford, Blackwell, 1986).
17. There is also a posthumous volume, *Papers on Logic and Ethics*, edited by Peter Geach and A.J. Kenny (London, 1976).

CHAPTER 10
RETIREMENT WITH PHILOSOPHERS AND FRIENDS IN CAMBRIDGE: RICHARD BRAITHWAITE AND MARGARET MASTERMAN

1. See *Early Fathers from the Philokalia*, pp. 17–18: translated by E. Kadloubovsky and G.E.H. Palmer (London, Faber, 1944).
2. I went into this in an article 'Theoria and the Way of Life' in *The Journal of Theological Studies* N.S. Vol *XVII*, Pt. 1, 1966.
3. My account of Richard Braithwaite is based on the address I gave at his Memorial Service in King's College Chapel on 26 May 1990. I am grateful to the Provost of King's for permission to use this.
4. He was a stricter empiricist than either Margaret or myself, but happy to discuss metaphysical views if any reasons could be produced in support of them.
5. There are still some copies left, and I shall be glad to give one to anyone who knew Margaret and writes to ask for it.
6. The title of my book was *The Role of the Unrealisable*.

CHAPTER 11
RETROSPECT AND PROSPECT

1. In particular, in *The Moral Roots of Social Democracy*, Tawney Society Publications, No. 26, ed. Tony Flowers (1985).
2. A.N. Whitehead, *Religion in the Making*, pp. 39–40 (Cambridge, 1927).
3. See especially C.H. Waddington, *Towards a Theoretical Biology* 2, pp. 72–81 (Edinburgh, 1969).
4. 'Coleridge on the Growth of the Mind'. Originally a lecture given in the John Rylands Library, Manchester (Bulletin XXXIV, 2, March 1952).
5. For instance by Kathleen Coburn in *Coleridge: a Collection of Critical Essays* (Prentice Hall, N.J., 1967).
6. 2 *Corinthians* 4.8. Rob Sawers pointed out to me the metaphor in *poros*.

Index